2 Wk

turn n or before

14

2016

COUNSELLING
• IN ACTION •

Series editor: Windy Dryden

Counselling in Action is a series of books developed especially for counsellors and students of counselling which provides clear and explicit guidelines for counselling practice. A special feature of the series is the emphasis it places on the *process* of counselling.

Titles include:

Feminist Counselling in Action
Jocelyn Chaplin

Gestalt Counselling in Action
Petrūska Clarkson

Integrative Counselling Skills in Action
Sue Culley

Key Issues for Counselling in Action
Edited by Windy Dryden

Training and Supervision for Counselling in Action
Edited by Windy Dryden and Brian Thorne

Personal Construct Counselling in Action
Fay Fransella and Peggy Dalton

Psychodynamic Counselling in Action
Michael Jacobs

Experiences of Counselling in Action
Edited by Dave Mearns and Windy Dryden

Person-Centred Counselling in Action
Dave Mearns and Brian Thorne

Transactional Analysis Counselling in Action
Ian Stewart

Cognitive-Behavioural Counselling in Action
Peter Trower, Andrew Casey and Windy Dryden

FEMINIST
COUNSELLING
IN *Action*

JOCELYN CHAPLIN

SAGE Publications
London · Thousand Oaks · New Delhi

© Jocelyn Chaplin 1988

First published 1988
Reprinted 1990, 1991, 1992, 1993, 1995

All rights reserved. No part of this publication may be reproduced, stored in a retrieval system, transmitted or utilized in any form or by any means, electronic, mechanical, photocopying, recording or otherwise, without permission in writing from the Publishers.

SAGE Publications Ltd
6 Bonhill Street
London EC2A 4PU

SAGE Publications Inc
2455 Teller Road
Thousand Oaks, California 91320

SAGE Publications India Pvt Ltd
32, M-Block Market
Greater Kailash – I
New Delhi 110 048

British Library Cataloguing in Publication Data

Chaplin, Jocelyn
  Feminist counselling in action. –
  (Counselling in action).
  1. Feminist counselling
  I. Title   II. Series
  361.3'23

ISBN 0–8039–8079–5
ISBN 0–8039–8080–9 Pbk

Library of Congress catalog card number 88–061056

Typeset by Fakenham Photosetting Ltd, Fakenham, Norfolk
Printed in Great Britain by J.W. Arrowsmith Ltd, Bristol

Contents

Preface   vii

Acknowledgements   ix

1   Introduction   1

2   Setting the Scene   18

3   Getting Started and Building Trust:
the Mothering Phase   28

4   Identifying Themes: Separating out
the Opposites   44

5   Exploring the Past: Understanding the
Opposites and Inner Hierarchies   56

6   Dissolving the Inner Hierarchies and Facing
Ambivalence: Accepting the Opposites   71

7   Making Changes: Living with the Opposites   85

8   Assertiveness Training: Expressing
the Opposites   98

9   Standing Up on Both Feet: Endings
and New Beginnings   111

References   125

Index   127

SHREWSBURY COLLEGE LIBRARY

INV. No. 5979754   7/2/97

ORD No. 17349   10/1/97

ACC No.   018993

CLASS No.

PRICE £10.95   CHECKED

This book is dedicated to my daughter Rosita,
who has taught me so much

Preface

When first asked to write about feminist counselling I felt that I was being faced with an impossible task. I had often heard colleagues arguing that there is no such thing as feminist counselling or therapy, only 'good' practice which can be carried out by people with a feminist ideology in more or less the same way as those with different ideologies. Certainly there is not one set of techniques that can be labelled 'feminist', but there is a general approach, a way of thinking. It includes such common factors as an anti-hierarchical stance, awareness of cyclical and rhythmical processes, the interconnection of opposites and a recognition of the deep influence of society on everyone's psyche.

I can only write about my particular experience of feminist counselling. I look at feminist counselling through my own specific set of assumptions and experiences, through my own 'spectacles', yet I do hope that many people will empathize with at least some of the experiences, values and ways of thinking that I describe, and find them stimulating even when they disagree.

Acknowledgements

This book would not have been possible without the many clients with whom I have had the privilege of working, and from whom I have learnt so much. First, I want to thank them all for their courage and honesty in letting me walk with them for a while on their personal journeys of self-discovery.

I thank, too, all the students on the psychology, anthropology and counselling courses that I have taught over the years, for their openness to new ideas. I must also express my appreciation of their willingness to share personal experiences that gave flesh and blood to the bare bones of the theories.

In many ways I feel that this book has not been written just by me, but is rather the product of five years of weekly peer supervision with Sara Gibson and Mildred Levious. Time and time again as I wrote, I could hear the three of us in discussion. I owe many of my insights to Mildred and Sara. I also want to thank them for encouraging me and for continuing to have faith in me even when I had lost my own. I want to thank Brigid Proctor who has been our friend and supervisor, sharing her wisdom and giving us invaluable support. Brigid's encouragement and interest in this book gave me the confidence to write for the counselling field in general as well as specifically for feminists.

I would also like to thank Amelie Noak for helping me clarify ideas about opposites and Penny Cloutte for helping me make connections between feminism and the rhythm model. Without Windy Dryden, who asked me to write this book, it would never have happened. I want to thank him for the enormous amount of time and effort he has put into editing it. I also thank Ginny England for typing the manuscript. I would like to acknowledge all those friends and colleagues who have supported and encouraged me through my writing, in particular Ruth Popplestone, Chantal Baker, Diedre Parinder, Clare Walsh, Jenni Johnson, John Rowan, Christine Haggert, Michael Spurgeon and Joan Miller.

Finally I thank my mother for giving me an invaluable independence of mind, and my daughter Rosita for being so understanding about the many hours spent away from her, working on the book.

1 Introduction

Feminism is not merely an issue,
but rather a new mode of being.

(Daly, 1986: 113)

I often meet people interested in counselling who say, 'I'm not a feminist but . . .' They then go on to reveal an interest in just the kinds of ideas explored in this book. It is written for them as well as for feminist counsellors, trainees and any other counsellors who think the feminist approach might be useful in their practice. Rather than giving detailed instruction on 'how to be a feminist counsellor', I have focused on the processes that clients go through, discussing the counsellor's role in each phase.

The book is also written for feminists and others who may have been deeply suspicious of the whole therapy/counselling world for its generally patriarchal and hierarchical attitudes. As we shall see, feminism questions all forms of hierarchy including those between counsellors and clients.

This first chapter is a general introduction to the basic concepts involved in feminist counselling as I understand and practise it, and an overview of what is involved. Although the concepts are fundamental to the practice, some readers may prefer to start by reading Chapters 3 to 9, which deal with the counselling process itself and include examples. The first chapter could be read later as a way of bringing together the various themes.

Chapter 2 deals with some of the initial aspects of the counselling process: Who comes? How does a counsellor reach potential clients? Where do we work? How do we charge? What do we say at the very first meeting?

The rest of the book follows seven typical phases of a counselling cycle, each chapter covering one aspect. In my experience, not all clients move through all seven phases within the same counselling contract of, say, a year with one counsellor. It may take them many years to go through the cycle, or it may take just a few weeks. They may use several different counsellors, workshops or 'spiritual' guides during their growth cycle. And most people seem to go through many cycles during their lifetime.

At the same time, however, the different elements of each phase may recur in later phases, being woven together as people change and develop. Clients rarely move in straight lines from 1 to 7, but because making books is a somewhat linear form of expression, I have presented the stages as a sequence of chapters. I have not separated theory and practical aspects in a linear way, but woven them together throughout the book, to show how they interconnect.

In addition to exploring the theory and practice of each phase of counselling, I also describe the cycles of three specific clients. These are all women, although in my experience men seem to move through the same phases and share many of the issues that women have to face. But some specific issues affect women differently from men. The emphasis in this book is on women's development process, although male clients are mentioned from time to time. The three example clients are from different class backgrounds, begin heterosexual and are fairly representative of the range of clients likely to come for counselling in any country where it is available. In my experience with black and white clients from several different cultures, the same kinds of general human issues seem to be important to everyone. However there are specific issues that relate to particular cultures and not to others. There are also issues around racism that affect black clients differently from white clients. However these particular kinds of differences and their effects on the counselling process are described in another book in this series (d'Ardenne) and will not be explored in detail here. Yet I am aware that as a white, middle class English woman many of my assumptions and linguistic expressions are specific to my particular culture and background.

The three clients, Julia, Mary and Louise, are actually fictional characters made up from a number of different clients, students and friends. Any potentially revealing details have been changed, for the sake of confidentiality.

What is Feminist Counselling?

Feminist counselling is not just a technique or style. There is no school of feminist counselling. For me it is about a different way of being, having different attitudes to each other and different values and ways of thinking. Feminist counselling is not only about living more fully in the present, like most other forms of counselling. It is also about working towards the future. It is training people, men as well as women, for a society that does not yet exist; a society in which so-called 'feminine' values and ways of thinking are valued as much as so-called 'masculine' ones.

'Feminine' and 'masculine' are words that are burdened by so many layers of socially constructed meaning that I would prefer not to use them at all, so when I do they have inverted commas round them to remind us of their limitations. Yet the words 'female' and 'male' imply some kind of rigid biological determinism that I also reject. This book does, however, stress real differences in ways of thinking that thousands of years of patriarchy have associated with females and males respectively. It does not mean that male people are genetically incapable of using ways of thinking previously associated mainly with female people, or vice versa.

Broadly speaking, the way of thinking associated with males separates out elements of a situation into distinct categories. It then tends to focus on one element as opposed to the other. It may involve a competition between them in which one must eventually win. In everyday terms it could be seen as prioritizing, as between home and work. One element is chosen and the other rejected. This way of thinking is a necessary part of life, but if taken to extremes, it means that everything gets *permanently* divided into superior and inferior, for example, work is always seen as superior to home. It becomes rigidly hierarchical, as are most patriarchal societies.

On the other hand, the way of thinking associated with females stresses the interconnection of elements in a situation and can allow movement from one to the other at different times. If taken to extremes it can involve a one-sided rejection of difference and separateness. Yet because the 'female' model allows for its own opposite, the 'male' model, it can itself contain both of them, in their non-extreme forms.

There are also values which have become associated with females and males respectively. For instance, asserting our individual needs and goals has become associated with males and caring for others with females. Both these values are important and necessary, for women and for men, but in a patriarchal society the values associated with females are viewed as permanently inferior. Feminist counselling is helping to prepare people for a society in which nurturing and co-operation are respected as much as independence and assertiveness.

Feminist counselling rejects the prevailing hierarchical model of thinking in which one 'side' must always win. It recognizes the interconnection between different, even opposite, sides of life and of ourselves. This is a totally different approach from the one on which most of our modern thinking is based, in which we are taught to strive all the time for set goals and to move in *one* direction up a hierarchical ladder. The feminist counselling model is more like a spiral path that goes backwards as well as forwards through many cycles of development and fulfilment. We can move between our conscious and our unconscious, our joy and our sorrow, our activity and our rest, our 'inner' and 'outer' worlds.

This emphasis on the interconnections between things and people is related to ecology and alternative holistic medicine, to new age spirituality and humanistic psychology. It is also related to other 'progressive' movements in the world that are struggling towards greater justice and equality. It is about respecting and celebrating differences such as female/male, black/white, as opposed to the present view of difference that is concerned with superiority and inferiority, winning or losing, or flat denial of difference altogether. Feminist counselling is profoundly social and political as well as personal and individual.

In common with the radical therapies of the 1970s (Steiner, 1975), an essential feature of *feminist* counselling is our recognition of the deep interconnectedness of our 'internal' psychological worlds with the 'external' social and material worlds. At present, our psyches as well as our bodies are affected by life in a competitive hierarchical society. In particular we are aware of the impact of 'second-class' status and gender stereotyping on women's psyches and on the way we think about ourselves and others. But we also recognize the damage that masculine stereotyping has done to male psychologies.

Feminist counselling is also concerned with the profound influence of other social hierarchies such as race and class, sexual orientation and disability. In addition to economic disadvantage, certain groups of people are made to feel inadequate and inferior in many different ways. In place of hierarchical thinking, we help people to value all sides of themselves. Different characteristics can be used at different times. We can alternate through time, for example being strong one day and vulnerable the next. In the same way, we believe that society could use and value differences between groups, rather than defining one group as permanently superior to and in charge of the other. No one part of ourselves, such as our 'head', need always be in control of another part, such as our 'heart'. Many people come into counselling terrified of letting go the rigid control that they consider their 'heads' must have over their 'bodies and emotions'.

The 'Feminine' Rhythm Model versus the 'Masculine' Control Model

Throughout this book the concepts of rhythm and the interconnection of opposites will come up. I work with a model of life (the 'rhythm model') which helps to make sense of the world and our own selves, and is fundamentally different to the model which is generally unthinkingly accepted in society, which I call the 'control model'. A model is essentially a simplified image of the way we perceive the world, a kind of half-way stage between 'inner' imagination and 'outer' reality. The 'rhythm' and 'control' models are two contrasting ways of seeing relationships between people and things. They are

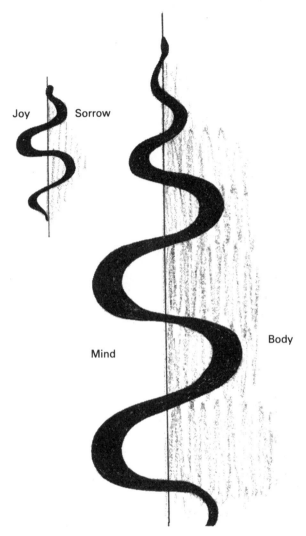

Figure 1   *The rhythm model*

also the underlying supporting structures for two very different kinds of ideology, one pro-equality and the other pro-hierarchy.

Unconsciously we use the control, hierarchical model most of the time, at least in Western cultures. But we rarely visualize it as a concrete image. Figure 2 shows the control model in a simple two-dimensional form. The opposites are split hierarchically, and the model is shown as a pyramid. The shape is arrow-like, yet static. It

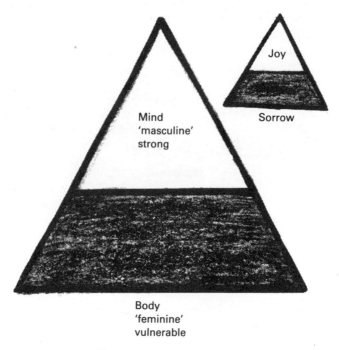

Figure 2   *The control model*

suggests a climb upwards towards the peak, the success, the goal or even God. But the upward-thrusting movement is frozen in its tracks. It is fossilized. The pyramid is a powerful image of hierarchy, with the minority at the top ruling the majority at the bottom.

Figure 1 shows the rhythm model, which has a far greater sense of movement, change and life itself. The movement is from one opposite side to another. It can be seen as motion through time, as a dance or even a struggle arising from the tensions between the opposites. When one movement has reached an extreme, there is a swing back to another one. It is a kind of balancing mechanism that we know goes on throughout nature. Yet perfect, permanent balance is never achieved, for that would be the end of the dance, or death. The path of the rhythm could be seen as the path taken by a person who experienced first joy and then sorrow, first strength, then vulnerability at different times of one day or one lifetime. And then at some stage they return to the first state, and so on. It is a model describing the alternation process that connects the opposites through time. It has been described as the 'feminine mode' (Perera, 1981): 'Alternation, the oscillating way, is a function of the feminine self.'

How Does the Non-hierarchical Rhythmic Model Affect our Practice?

Feminist counsellors are committed to transforming hierarchical relationships into more egalitarian ones, whether these be in society at large or in the consulting room. But what about the counsellor-client relationship? Isn't that inevitably hierarchical? No. Too often equality gets confused with sameness. The client and the counsellor are not the same; they have separate and different roles. But the counsellor is not there to dominate or have power over the client. Women and others at the bottom of hierarchies usually have enough experience in their everyday lives of being dominated or put down, and the low self-esteem resulting from such experience is often what brings them to counselling in the first place. Feminist counselling aims instead to empower people and help them develop more self-confidence and control over their own lives. The counsellor is not seen as the expert or the doctor; the client is not a patient. Rather they are two different people using 'clues' to explore the life of one of them. The focus is on the client. The counsellor is not there to explore her own life. Her role is one of container, supporter and enabler. 'Containing' here means being present with the client in a firm but accepting way and not being afraid of strong feelings. The client's role is one of self-exploration. Neither counsellor nor client is superior.

It is however important to remember that when some clients first come into counselling, they are coming in with the old hierarchical ways of thinking deeply ingrained. They expect to be told what to do. They are looking for Mummy and Daddy. As feminist counsellors we try to respect clients' present reality as we help them to develop alternative 'ways of seeing'. We may accept the parent role initially until the client learns to do without it.

Dealing with 'Objective' and 'Subjective' Realities

We also respect and acknowledge the 'objective' realities of the client's life as well as the 'subjective' inner world of her thoughts and feelings. Subjective and objective are seen as two more interconnected opposites, though of course we recognize the problems involved in separating the two. For example, a woman client who was unable to work effectively in the office because of her rage against a male boss would have her objective situation taken seriously. Events are often 'seen' from a male viewpoint, so that the experience of women is made to seem less 'real', less 'valid'. Feminist counselling should never belittle a client's view of her experience. The angry woman would, however, be encouraged to divide the situation into 'objective' and 'subjective' aspects. On the objective side would be the detailed realities of what the boss actually says and does that offends her. It would include the structure of the office hierarchy and the roles men and women are expected to play. The subjective side would involve expressing her own feelings and thoughts about the situation and making connections with other similar situations, possibly in her childhood.

For example, the behaviour she cannot stand might include being touched invasively while talking about business. This touching is objective harassment. But on the subjective side she may be letting it happen because she is too scared to say 'no' to it. To deal with objective realities she might be encouraged to take action through her union if there is one, but she would also be encouraged to act more assertively towards the boss. She might have to practise new more assertive behaviour with the counsellor many times before she feels comfortable acting it out in the office.

On the subjective side, she might be finding it especially difficult to be assertive with her boss because her father used to behave in a similar way when she was a child. And some (but not all) of her present rage comes from the past and from unexpressed anger towards her father. Feminist counsellors can work on both levels. We are concerned with 'external' behaviour change as well as 'internal' changes to feelings and thoughts. Experience has shown that the two levels are closely interconnected. When a woman starts behaving more assertively, she generally starts feeling more confident and self-accepting inside.

As well as expressing feelings such as anger towards others such as her father, the client also needs to learn new ways of thinking. Thought and feeling are also interconnected. Women being harassed in the office, for example, often feel that it is their fault. And yet male bosses misusing their power over female employees is an old social problem, stemming from the power hierarchies of male dominance over females in general. Putting the blame outside oneself can be a vital stage in counselling. But there is also the need to think more positively about ourselves. Most women have low self-esteem. Valuing oneself and being in touch with what we really want, and then 'going for it' assertively all has to be learnt, or relearnt. Most little girls are brought up to value males more than themselves and to live through and for others rather than being self-directed.

So learning new patterns of behaviour and thinking is as important as working with the psychodynamics of deep unconscious emotions. Like everything else in feminist counselling, it is not a matter of 'either/or', one *or* the other way of working. One technique does not have to win over another, but one can illuminate and help the other.

The Social Unconscious: our Assumptions about Ourselves

Learnt social attitudes such as 'females should be passive and caring while males should be aggressive and competitive' are as deeply buried in the unconscious as our early personal experiences. Ideas about a male god with ultimate power over everything have a profound effect on our unconscious feelings about men and women, and about fathers and male authority figures in particular. Imagine how differently we would feel if our image of God was female!

The control or hierarchical model of life is firmly planted in our social unconscious and affects our attitudes and feelings towards almost everything. It operates in subtle as well as obvious ways. For example, we unconsciously assume that the mind is superior to the body. This leads us to feel that we should be able to control everything with our minds. It may even encourage us to despise our bodies. Another example is the way that strength is valued over weakness and vulnerability, so we all try to hide our vulnerable sides. Many women today are trying to be 'super-woman', holding families and jobs together, feeling totally responsible for everyone around them. While this can seem like powerfulness, eventually many such women are exhausted by the one-sided life they lead. Fear of weakness or of 'letting go' can result in having no space for oneself or never allowing others to do the nurturing. A more rhythmic way of living where we take care of others sometimes, and let them take care of us at other times, is far more healthy.

For many men, fear of weakness is also disastrous psychologically, as it encourages the hiding and even ignoring of feelings. Feelings of any kind can be seen as weakness. 'Big boys don't cry' is a stereotyped example of this particular hierarchical attitude.

Most of us have hierarchies of acceptable and unacceptable sides of ourselves. Jungian therapists call the unacceptable side 'the shadow'. And in our culture there are deep hierarchical assumptions about darkness (black) as bad and light (white) as good. Counselling often involves learning to accept and even see the 'good' in the shadow. One client saw her rational side as cold and calculating. She wanted to get rid of it altogether. Its opposite, the feeling side, was seen as all good. In counselling she was able to see both sides as valuable, both having their strengths and weaknesses. I have often found that the very thing we call our weakness can also be our greatest strength.

The hierarchical way of thinking can turn even our personal growth into a 'win or lose' situation. One side must 'win' over the other and get rid of the loser. Many people feel that their 'good' grown-up responsible side must win over their 'bad' child-like irresponsible side. In feminist counselling we try to help clients accept and develop all sides of themselves as equally valuable in different ways. Instead of the so-called 'masculine' hierarchical thinking, we encourage what has sometimes been called the 'feminine' mode of knowing (Hall, 1980). This is an ancient wisdom recognizing the interconnectedness of opposites such as light and dark, joy and sorrow and the way they alternate through time. For example, instead of trying to get rid of sadness altogether and be 'happy' all the time, we see it as part of the emotional cycles of life. Indeed the very things that make us most happy are usually the source of our sorrow too. Only when sadness is not allowed does it fester inside, and all too often turn into depression.

As a feminist counsellor I recognize that we need a balance between the so-called 'masculine' and 'feminine' sides of ourselves. We are concerned with developing and valuing the largely ignored, devalued 'feminine' characteristics in everyone, including men and in society as a whole. The very word 'feminine' has connotations of weakness and inferiority today. We reject these associations, and stress that characteristics previously associated with females, such as caring, empathy, recognizing interconnections, containing, cooperating and being in touch with cyclical change, are available to everyone. They are also desperately needed by modern society everywhere in these overly competitive times.

The Roots of Feminist Counselling

Four main influences have shaped the development of modern feminist counselling: (1) The ancient roots of 'feminine wisdom'; (2) modern feminism; (3) psychoanalysis; (4) humanistic psychology.

The Ancient Roots of 'Feminine' Wisdom

Pre-historical mythology has provided many insights which have been integrated into the development of feminist counselling. Although archaeological and mythical evidence is limited, many scholars (Graves, 1955; Stone, 1976; Gimbutas, 1982; Melaart, 1967) have argued that the idea of cyclical or rhythmic action and thinking was a predominant approach in the neolithic and perhaps even paleolithic cultures of the near East, Africa, Asia and Europe. Many ancient religions seem to have been based on the great cycles and rhythms of nature, involving a sense of the interconnection of all things that we have since lost. Neolithic people seem to have had an awareness of the importance of death as well as life, of decay as well as growth, of destruction as well as creation. Just as the seasons change from spring to summer, to winter and then the rebirth of spring again, so their religious symbols followed the same patterns.

Some of these symbols and images can be useful to us today in our own psychological cycles, to help us understand ourselves better and to grow and change. We do not need to 'worship' those ancient images, or even to believe in a long-lost 'matriarchal paradise' for them to help us in the here and now.

One early image was that of the twin goddess who both gave life and took it away. She belonged to both the overworld and the underworld and could alternate between them, like Innana of Summer, or Persephone of Greece. In Catal Huyuk (Melaart, 1967) around 6,000 BC many shrines had double-headed goddesses. Another early form was that of the triple goddess; she is depicted in three main aspects. She is the young maiden — Spring (Persephone), the fertile mother — Summer (Demeter) and the wise old woman — Winter (Hecate). It seems (Graves, 1955) that originally all three were viewed as aspects of the same god/goddess.

Another form or image that was commonly associated with ancient 'feminine' wisdom was that of the snake and its symbol, the spiral. Many of us are familiar with the images of Minoan snake goddesses discovered in Crete, which date back to about 1,600 BC. The Minoan civilization seems to have been one of the last cultures based on goddess worship and respect for women, at least in Europe before the take-over by more patriarchal (e.g. Hellenic) tribes. But the snake had been a powerful religious symbol for many thousands of years before the Minoan period. It was a major feature of the art and religion of Old Europe 6,300–3,500 BC as described by Gimbutas (1982: 94):

> The snake and its abstracted derivative the spiral, are the dominant motifs of the art of Old Europe ... the mysterious dynamism of the snake, its extraordinary vitality and periodic rejuvenation must have provoked a powerful emotional response in the Neolithic agriculturalists, and the snake was consequently mythologised, attributed with a power that can move the entire cosmos.

It seemed to represent the rhythms of the eternal life-force itself as it curls and spirals through the universe. It appears as the primordial form of nature herself as she emerges out of chaos.

Many ancient creation myths refer to the origin of the world as being associated with a snake or serpent, for example, Orphion and Tiamet (Graves, 1955). Yet later myths, of patriarchal Babylon, for example, depict the slaying of the serpent. In Babylon, Tiamet was killed and cut up by her son Murduk; in the Judeo-Christian traditions, the serpent is shown as evil rather than as a symbol of valuable 'female' wisdom in the story of Adam and Eve.

It is interesting to note here that the spiral model has been used for thousands of years, even after the rise of patriarchal religions, as a symbol of the journey of the soul. It retained a psychological significance long after it lost its religious importance (Purce, 1974). It still represented the power of human nature to transform itself, to change and to grow between opposites. To this day it is retained as a symbol of healing, for example on the emblem of the British Medical Association. In the past it was women who were mainly associated with the power of healing of both body and mind. In the pre-historic world priestesses seem to have been the most powerful spiritual leaders, healers and guides of their communities (Graves, 1955). (It seems likely that many of them played the role of counsellor.) And even right through into the Middle Ages 'wise women' were still seen as having special powers and knowledge of healing (English and Ehrenreich, 1979).

The rise of 'science' in the last three hundred years seemed to destroy the older ideas of holism and natural rhythms, but recently scientific disciplines have come to accept the relative nature of many phenomena. They now seem to be leading us right back to the old concept of interconnected opposites, constant change and transformation, rhythm and the self-regulation of the universe (Capra, 1975). Only this time we can understand the 'serpent' with our conscious analytical minds. One way of achieving this is using the rhythm model to think differently about ourselves and the world we live in.

This model also has connections with the dialectical world view of Marx and Engels. 'Dialectical thought is only the reflection of the motion through opposites which asserts itself everywhere in nature, and which by the continual conflict of the opposites, and their final passage into one another, or into higher forms, determines the life of nature' (Engels, 1934: 211).

Modern Feminism

Many modern feminists were influenced by the political ideals of Marxism and socialism, especially in Europe. The most recent Feminism grew partly out of the struggles for equality, civil rights, people's power etc. in the 1960s. Many women became active in fighting other people's oppression before turning their attention to the oppression of women. While for some the more 'spiritual' side of women's power became the focus, for others it was the political aspects of feminism that took first place. Today there is an increasing interconnection of these two major strands. Thinking and action can't be separated.

Although women have been struggling against their oppression in many ways for thousands of years, it is this modern wave of feminism that has provided much of the consciousness underlying feminist counselling. There have been important books (De Beauvoir, 1960; Friedan, 1977; Greer, 1971; Firestone, 1979; Baker-Miller, 1978; Daly, 1986; Chodorow, 1978; Berlotti, 1977; Chesler, 1972), but the movement has developed just as much through women getting together in consciousness-raising or active groups. In such groups women have come to their own personal understandings of how society's structures, attitudes and actions have depowered them. And feminist counselling has grown out of such groups and such understandings, as women have wanted to explore more deeply the effects of society on their psyches. Often this has led women, and men too, into one-to-one counselling, where they may feel safer to explore difficult feelings.

Yet in the early 1970s many feminists rejected psychoanalysis as a vehicle for these explorations (e.g. Firestone, 1979). They argued that it often seemed more concerned to socialize women into their roles as wives and mothers than to encourage them to take control of their own lives. Indeed many psychoanalysts are still making unconscious assumptions about women's needs and roles. We cannot, however, ignore the useful insights of psychoanalysis because some aspects of it have been mistaken or not fully thought out. Since the 1970s further work has been done which incorporates modern feminist thinking more effectively into psychoanalytical thinking.

Psychoanalysis
Freud's attempts to understand the dynamics of the unconscious certainly opened the way for a great increase in human self-understanding and the growth of a vast range of therapies. Many of Freud's followers, such as Karen Horney (1924), offered considerable insight into women's thinking. While Freud argued that women's envy of men resulted from their lack of a penis, Horney recognized that any envy was as much to do with men's greater power and status in society as to do with their physical attributes. She was one of the first psychoanalysts to combine her understanding of the unconscious with an awareness of the impact of social factors such as power structures.

During the 1970s more and more psychoanalysts were able to incorporate feminism into their practice. This process was aided by the publication of Juliet Mitchell's book on psychoanalysis and feminism, in which she used many of Freud's insights to help women understand why, despite consciousness-raising, so many of us were still stuck in self-defeating patterns (Mitchell, 1975).

Some interesting developments of this combination of feminism and psychoanalysis have been explored by Orbach and Eichenbaum (1982), who set up the Women's Therapy Centre in London. They used psychoanalytic theory to look at the relationships of baby girls to their mothers, and how these differ from those of little boys. They noticed that separation from mother is often more problematic for girls, who are more likely to be closely identified with their mothers. They also noted that while most men have their dependency needs met by women, mothers, wives and girlfriends (who are *expected* to do the nurturing), women's similar needs are rarely satisfied. They see one role of the therapist as a 're-mothering'. Counsellors as well as psychoanalysts often seem to have this role. We can fully accept the client without making judgements, as their real mothers may have done.

Nevertheless there are important differences between counselling and psychoanalysis. Although feminists are committed to an anti-hierarchical ideology, this may be more difficult to put into practice in a traditional psychoanalytic relationship. The psychoanalytic therapist has to play the role of parent in order for the client to transfer her childhood feelings on to her. This strong emphasis on transference is a major difference between psychoanalysis and other kinds of therapy. The generally long-term and intense (three or four times a week) nature of psychoanalytic therapy process tends to encourage a child-like dependence that may often be necessary for the client's growth process, but not all clients need this kind of relationship in order to grow and understand themselves better.

Counselling tends to be shorter-term: six months or a year or even less. Clients are more likely to come only once a week. There is more likely to be a peer relationship in which the experience is of two equal adults talking to each other. This does not mean that a counsellor does not also often play a parenting role, though they vary between that and an 'equal' one. Counsellors also use many of the insights contributed by Freud and other therapists and analysts. They frequently work with material related to early childhood experiences and dreams, and explore the relationship between counsellor and client.

Another difference between counselling and psychoanalytic therapy is that in addition to helping many clients explore their unconscious motivations and behaviour patterns, counsellors often work with present, practical issues. Counsellors may spend time helping clients to work out career choices, for example. A counsellor might use assertion training techniques to help a client prepare for a difficult interview. The counsellor takes present reality as seriously as the past influences. She may spend time looking at the objective, material conditions of the client's life today, such as her housing problems.

Humanistic Psychology

Feminist counselling owes as much to the humanistic psychology tradition as to the insights of psychoanalysis. Humanistic approaches to human growth developed in the USA in the 1950s and 60s partly in reaction to the length, expense and hierarchical nature of psychoanalysis. But they were also influenced by Eastern philosophies, e.g. Taoism, that had a much more rhythmic view of life, similar in some ways to the religions of the neolithic world. There was more emphasis on living in the present, on 'being' rather than 'having' or 'doing'. Humanistic counsellors and therapists are less concerned with the past and early childhood than with living in the 'here and now' and fulfilling our human potential. They have a more optimistic view of human nature, and are holistic in approach, dealing with the whole person; the body and mind are seen as equally important.

Their techniques are often more active and directive. Examples of humanistic approaches are Gestalt, transactional analysis and rebirthing. Their methods can often lead to reliving and understanding early childhood experiences through a caring confrontation that does not necessarily involve interpretation.

It is suitable for people who just want to get more out of life as well as those with specific 'problems'. There is a belief in people taking control of their own lives, and counselling sessions too for that matter. Many humanistic psychologists are committed to equality, and encourage self-help groups and self-reliance.

Many feminist counsellors and therapists prefer to use a humanistic approach (Brown and Liss-Levinson, 1981; Forisba, 1981), as it seems to be less inevitably hierarchical, but we do not need to stick to just one approach.

As a feminist counsellor I feel that I am a weaver in the subtle hidden threads that make up the fabric of human development. We can weave in and out of unconscious depths, and in and out of all the different techniques and approaches to counselling and therapy. Feminist counselling is a process, not one technique or theory. I can allow myself to make connections between different approaches, finding similarities as well as differences, taking what is useful and leaving what feels oppressive.

The Social Limits of Feminist Counselling

Feminist counselling is not only about recognizing the importance of gender in psychology. It involves such a totally different way of thinking about everything that it is difficult to define in our available language and hierarchical thought patterns and social structures. It does not fit comfortably with existing society. For example, while we still have patriarchal marriages, feminist counselling is limited in its effectiveness. While we still have a profit-seeking, hierarchical economy we can only expect to achieve a limited independence for women. While we still have stereotyped, hierarchical images of each other we can only go so far in helping people to change.

It is difficult to be 'healthy' in an 'unhealthy' society. And many so-called neurotic patterns that people bring to counselling are vital survival mechanisms in an 'unhealthy' society. Baker-Miller (1978) makes this point especially in relation to women, whose very strengths are labelled weaknesses by patriarchal society. There are so many contradictory messages being conveyed to women today. 'Be caring as women are supposed to, *but* being caring is being weak.' 'Be strong, and hold your family together, but be weak and soft as "feminine" women are supposed to be.' No wonder so many of us are 'neurotic'. In fact we need to respect the various ingenious ways that we have coped rather than see them as personal failings. Far too often women blame themselves for problems that are not of their own making. By helping them to see the processes actually at work, during counselling, we contribute to their ability to deal with them more effectively and thus contribute to changes in society.

Varieties of Feminist Counselling Techniques

All feminist counsellors would agree that social structures, such as our limited gender expectations and women's second-class status, affects both our psychology and that of men. But the ways in which we work with actual clients vary. Some are more psychoanalytically orientated, others are humanistic. Some are influenced by Rogers (1951) whose client-centred approach fits well with feminist approaches to counselling. He stresses the power of empathy, warmth and unconditional positive regard, which have long been regarded as strengths learnt and developed more by women than men. (Skills like empathy and good listening are now being valued more in fields such as counselling and management training. When they were labelled 'feminine skills' they were dismissed and devalued while at the same time being taken for granted. Mothers and wives especially were automatically expected to be 'good at listening'.)

There are also behaviourally orientated feminist counsellors who believe that we *learn* unhelpful patterns of behaviour and thinking, such as always being passive or having racist attitudes, and that these are not innate. They can be 'unlearnt' and new patterns such as assertive behaviour can be learnt. Assertion-training courses are increasingly popular with women. But many counsellors also use assertion-training and assertive ways of thinking in their one-to-one work too. Assertion is mainly about being clear about what we really want and asking for it directly, while respecting the other person. It doesn't mean we always get what we want, but it is an approach to relationships based on equality and clarity rather than one based on hierarchy, dishonesty or confusion. It can be used in many different situations from the boardroom to the bedroom (Dickson, 1982).

Finally there are many feminist counsellors whose background is in Jungian psychology or related approaches. At one time Jung was dismissed by many feminists as being too mystical and retaining basic sexist assumptions about masculinity and femininity. But, as with other male-created theories and techniques, we can take what is useful and discard what is not. Feminists are developing their own ways of understanding and using the symbols and myths that Jung found so vital a part of our search for meaning. Women Jungians like Hall (1980) recognize that the Jungian model of interconnected opposites and the 'self-regulation' of the psyche is based on the ancient 'feminine way of knowing'. And despite Jung's own unconscious sexism he did appreciate the importance of the devalued so-called 'feminine' side of life. He also developed the concept of men having an anima (feminine soul) and women having an animus (masculine spirit).

Increasing numbers of feminist counsellors and therapists are using symbols in art therapy, guided fantasy, working with images, acting, drawing or dancing our own myths. These give form to our complex and often confusing feelings, hopes and fears, joys and sorrows. Counselling is about making journeys, inner journeys often through hazardous territory. Symbols can be seen as landmarks along the way. They can be used to focus and direct our energies. Dreams are of vital importance in these journeys, but their meanings are likely to be complex and changeable, occurring on many levels at once. Fixed static meanings for dream symbols are as alien to our model of thinking as any other rigid, one-sided, single-level interpretation of a symbol. Dreams can be used as starting-points for making connections, for the flow of imagination, for the stream of consciousness. The counsellor does not provide a static interpretation.

In addition to all the variety of theories and techniques used by feminist counsellors, there are also differences in our feminist ideology. We don't all need to share the same set of views. Socialist feminists, radical feminists, humanistic feminists, 'green' feminists and 'spiritual' feminists can all be successful counsellors, using their feminism in their counselling to whatever extent they feel comfortable with.

2   Setting the Scene

Some Vital Distinctions

Advice versus Counselling

One of the most effective ways of providing counselling has apparently been in connection with some other service, such as through doctors, welfare advisers etc. But in such situations it is vital that clear boundaries be created between advice-giving and counselling. In counselling we are creating a safe and supportive space for the client to explore and express feelings and thoughts, and perhaps be encouraged to consider alternative patterns, but we are not giving advice. We are not providing information about housing. In such situations it may be necessary to put on two different 'hats' with the same client. We can be advice-giver for one hour and counsellor for the next.

Many advice workers attend the training courses I run for people wanting to become counsellors. They want to use counselling skills in their work, but when they realize that counselling isn't about giving advice or 'rescuing' the client they come up against this conflict of roles. They need to use the two 'hats'.

Informal and Formal Counselling

The conflict between advice and counselling also relates to another conflict between informal and formal counselling. Lots of people with no formal training spend time listening to and advising friends on personal problems. This is especially true of women, whose way of life has usually traditionally included a lot of listening, support and concern with the emotional side of life.

But this book is about the more formal kind of counselling which involves clear boundaries of fifty-minute sessions and a definite difference in role between the person who is being counsellor and the client, even if they swap roles later, as in co-counselling. The kind of feminist counselling described in this book is done on a one-to-one basis, not in groups, while informal supportive counselling is often carried out in groups with no time-limits, and often no clearly defined roles. This kind of counselling is enormously valuable and without it many more women would suffer from depression and other neuroses. It enables us to share our problems and to realize that we are not alone. The more formalized consciousness-raising groups developed through the women's movement in the 1970s grew out of such supportive networks. In them women were able to share their frustrations as unfulfilled housewives and their rage with dominating and patronizing men, and to get in touch with their strengths and self-respect. Self-help groups of this kind are springing up everywhere among men as well as women, for people who share all kinds of problems from alcoholism to depression or for people with shared interests such as writing or parenting.

But the kind of counselling done in these groups is in a sense opposite to the kind of counselling I describe in this book. In the *informal group* the focus is on what we have in common and on what we share. Connections between people are more important than differences. The individual problem or personality is in the background. It doesn't go away; it is just not in focus. In *formal, individual counselling* the individual and her problem is focused on. It is in the foreground of the counselling arena. The shared experience of being women in a sexist society, of being sensitive in a hierarchical society, is there in the background. What we have in common does not go away; it is just not the main focus. We may even make comments from time to time, like 'Yes, it is difficult being a woman', or 'Many of us are brought up with those expectations', but as counsellors it is vital that we do not take away from clients the sense of their own importance and uniqueness by stressing their similarity with others too much. For in counselling they need to feel special. They should have the attention and unconditional acceptance that they may never have had as children. It is their space. And the counsellor is not there to share her feelings or thoughts.

Sometimes feminists have used the expression 'unconsciousness-raising' for therapy and counselling to distinguish it from 'consciousness-raising' which involves a more surface, cognitive experience. In 'unconsciousness-raising' or formal counselling, the focus is more on deep feelings and thoughts that may have been hidden away for years. Some of these feelings and thoughts may not be acceptable to some feminist consciousness-raising groups. For example, it can be difficult to admit feelings of dependency on a male partner or a longing to have babies or to be swept off one's feet by a strong man, etc. Yet these kinds of feelings are often around in the unconscious. They may not be 'ideologically correct' but they can still exist. Our 'unconsciouses' don't change as fast as our conscious ideology, or even as fast as social changes. Counselling of the formal one-to-one kind gives people a chance to admit to, and then explore, all these 'unacceptable' feelings and thoughts.

Another difference is that in formal counselling we encourage the client to stay with the feeling for as long as possible. We don't jump in to share that we 'Felt like that too' or to rescue them and say 'Oh, you shouldn't feel so bad.' That feeling belongs to the person expressing it. She has a right to that feeling. The desire to rescue is particularly strong for women (and for caring men), whose very identity can be so intimately linked to nurturing. We have learnt over many thousands of years to feel totally responsible for children and indeed for anyone seen as weak or helpless. We have been expected to 'hold' the family and everything else together. We are taught to feel that if anything goes wrong, especially emotionally, it is our fault. One of the hardest stages in counselling training is letting go of this sense of total responsibility and trusting the process of the client's growth itself.

Yet this relative detachment while counselling does not deny the value of nurturing, caring and empathy. Both approaches are needed, but at different times. In the same way people need *both* the support and connected sharing of the informal group *and* the space to concentrate on their own feelings. We do not see these two forms in terms of one or the other. Instead people can weave in and out of both types of counselling as each meets their needs at different times.

Referrals — or How do People find Counsellors and Who Comes?

Today most people come into counselling because they have a problem, but are not 'deeply' disturbed. Counsellors tend to see people who are 'normally neurotic', like most of us living in an abnormal society. In fact such labels as 'normal' are not often helpful. People come with problems in relationships, depression, lack of direction in life, a crisis, anxiety, weight problems. Most come of their own accord, possibly recommended by friends or colleagues. Some might be ex-mental patients referred by organizations, and a few are referred by doctors, other health professionals or alternative health practitioners such as acupuncturists.

Indeed increasingly links are being formed between counsellors and alternative health workers. Our approach to the client's own self-healing, self-regulating processes are very similar. We also have in common a concept of interconnected opposites; we all recognize the importance of balancing opposing energies in a rhythmic way, utilizing the idea of the spiral — the rhythm model described on p. 5. An increasing number of health centres are employing counsellors as part of a team that treats the whole person: body, mind and spirit. And the so-called 'spiritual' side of life is one in which more and more counsellors are becoming concerned. Many churches now provide counselling services — not to preach one religion or another, but to give people the space for their own growth.

Nevertheless most feminist counsellors prefer to work with women's centres, though the comparative lack of such centres means that many work privately from home. Some find their clients by advertising in feminist magazines, but naturally this approach is likely to attract only certain groups of women. Nevertheless many feminist women would prefer to see a feminist counsellor, so it is important to reach them.

The Influence of Class

Feminist counselling does not take place in a vacuum. It is embedded in a social and economic context, like all other forms of helping, and access to counselling is still largely much easier for the middle class. For most working-class people there usually has to be a 'serious mental problem', before counselling or therapy is sought.

Counsellors, especially if employed by the state, may be part of a controlling agency aimed at keeping working-class people in place. As feminist counsellors, they may want to encourage the expression of anger, encourage rebellion, encourage independence. Helping a woman stand on her own two feet may not fit in with some state agencies' assumptions about the woman's role in the family, and the counsellor is caught in a conflict between her values and those of the agency.

Another problem is that middle-class counsellors seeing working-class clients may be reinforcing the image (and reality) of the middle class being both in charge and more 'OK', with the working classes being 'the problem'. Although a feminist counsellor would recognize that the 'problem' is not the individual or even her class or culture, but the patriarchal class system as a whole, she isn't going to preach at her client. The client doesn't know what her 'political' attitudes are. All the counsellor can do is show through her attitude of respect towards the client that she does not see her as 'the problem' and does not look down on her in any way. It can also help if she does *not* work in a very middle-class environment.

It is important to make an effort to increase the availability of counselling as much as possible. Feminist counsellors and therapists are not alone in this attempt; indeed some of the earliest psychotherapists such as Adler (1956) and Reich (1970) deliberately chose to work in the poorer areas of Vienna and Berlin, and offered free treatment. There have been many examples of this approach since then, in Britain and the USA as well as elsewhere. Feminist counselling goes further, by making the interconnection of the 'personal' and 'political' one of its most central points. It is the recent women's movement that brought the slogan 'the personal is political' into the consciousness of mainstream modern society.

However, despite the efforts that have been made it is still the case that the majority of women who come for therapy, counselling or workshops are middle-class. Even those with working-class roots have usually been educated into the middle class, through university or college. This class difference is not only about economic differences. Indeed many middle-class clients are not well off, and may be living on the 'fringes' of society. But it is part of their middle-class culture to talk about feelings and about their 'inner' worlds. They are also more likely to know of other people who have been to counsellors. They are likely to read magazines where counselling and therapy is advertised. The problem of attracting working-class women to counsellors has yet to be effectively tackled.

First Impressions (Hidden Hierarchies in the Relationship)

Once the counsellor has been contacted, usually by phone, a whole range of impressions are created, through voice, accent, area and even the building where counselling is to take place. This is where the *social unconscious* comes in. The client is likely to make all kinds of assumptions such as 'If the counsellor lives in one district, they must be fairly left-wing; in another they must be middle-class; if they work in an alternative health centre they must have a humanistic orientation.' 'If they have a mid-European accent they must be analytically orientated and very wise!' A client could be put off by some of these factors unless they fit with their expectations. For example, some clients might have a previous image of a therapist as being someone old who talks slowly with a German accent, so a fast-talking young woman might feel wrong to them.

Many of us believe that by working at home and/or by disclosing little items of information about ourselves, that we are presenting ourselves as fallible human beings rather than as blank screens. But we also need to be very conscious of the impressions our homes or other places of work make on clients. For example, a room full of books is likely to tell the client that this person is very learned and academic. This could make some clients feel safe; that they are seeing someone who is an expert and has lots of knowledge, while others might feel inferior; so much less knowledgeable that the counselling could even decrease their self-esteem rather than increase it. So many of us have feelings of inferiority because of the academic hierarchies of the education system. On the other hand a very scruffy room in a run-down part of town might put off some clients. Many people think that counsellors should be 'totally together' people, with no problems, and immaculate homes and families. For some clients it is a relief to find that the counsellor is only human after all, but for others this is a threatening discovery. It depends partly on where the client is in terms of their own inner growth and development. At some stages they need to have a 'perfect parent' to look up to, and at other stages they need to see the counsellor as human, with negative sides as well as positive ones.

However we cannot keep changing our rooms according to which client is coming to see us, so we have to make decisions about how we are going to present ourselves. Do we have a few books, or a lot? Do we have photographs of our children, if we have any, around? What kind of clothes should we wear?

The only answer is that we must be authentic. We are presenting ourselves *as we are*, not as we think we should be. This can be a good model for the client.

We also need to be aware of feelings of envy in the client, for example, if we are living in more pleasant surroundings than they are. When she is ready such feelings can be expressed and explored in counselling. Clients' feelings about our other family members, such as children, are more likely to emerge if we work at home. They might feel jealous of our partners, as unconsciously they want us all to themselves. This too can be expressed when the client feels really trusting.

When we work in institutions, such as women's therapy centres, we consciously make the place as welcoming and pro-women as possible. As Ryan said, 'how different it is to walk into, say, the Women's Therapy Centre, compared to a conventional analytic institution, or medical clinic; the different social messages that are conveyed by the posters and notices on the walls or by the way you are likely to be addressed — formally or informally, seen as a patient or not' (Ryan, 1983). At a women's therapy centre women are not seen as patients. Their more informal attitude evokes a greater sense of equality than the hierarchical approach of most other institutions.

Because of our ingrained hierarchical thinking we often want our counsellors to sound like experts, which could lead us to expect strong, authoritative, possibly middle-class accents. Yet there is often an inner conflict between the unconscious search for the expert and resentment of their 'superior' status. We also crave equality. Many of us feel much more comfortable with someone to whom we feel equal, although we may take less seriously the insights offered by a 'more equal' counsellor than those suggested by one who is seen as superior. Our unconscious minds tend to see people largely in terms of status, and superior/inferior. As feminist counsellors we need to be constantly aware of the power of this hierarchical thinking.

But we also need to look at what we mean by 'equality' between counsellor and client. I have already said that we don't see ourselves as having a superior status, but does that mean that we have to be from similar backgrounds to our clients, and have similar personal circumstances, such as both being married or both being lesbians, or both having children? Clearly it would be extremely difficult to match everybody in such a way, but feminist counsellors do respect the desire of some lesbian clients to have lesbian counsellors and black women to have black counsellors if they choose. And where referral systems do exist, for example at a women's therapy centre, if a client asks for a particular kind of counsellor, her wish is complied with if possible, whereas some counselling organizations actually make it a policy not to comply with such wishes. They even argue that what a person asks for may be the opposite of what they need, on the assumption that the organization 'knows better'.

Most feminist counsellors recognize that it helps if they have themselves been through some of the same experiences as their clients. Indeed most of the basic issues that come up again and again in counselling are ones that all of us as humans have to grapple with at one stage or another. We all have to cope with losses and separations, with feelings of rejection and inadequacy, with questions of 'Who am I?' and 'Where am I going?' Even if we haven't experienced an actual bereavement, we should be able to work with a client who has been bereaved by drawing on our experience of other losses in life. In the sense that we are all human and share common fears and hopes, stages of life and vulnerabilities, we are equal. As feminist counsellors we need to keep reminding ourselves that we could easily be in that other chair being the client, and it is vital that we have our own therapy or counselling. We need to acknowledge our own weaknesses, hopes and fears so that we don't catch ourselves believing that we are OK and the client is not OK.

Aspects of Equality between Counsellor and Client

The first aspect of our equality is the human one of awareness of what we have in common. This attitude of mind is important for the counsellor, especially when meeting a client for the first time. For we too make our assumptions unconsciously about clients. They may come to us looking very unkempt, or anxious, and it would be easy to get into the 'I'm OK and they are not' pattern. So while we can use those first impressions as clues to their underlying patterns, we need also to respect the humanity that we both share.

The second aspect of equality is the specific fact that both are women in a male-dominated society. And even if our life circumstances are different, we have both suffered forms of 'put-down' or been patronized. Feminist counsellors do not preach feminism, but our awareness of the gender hierarchies is at the back of our minds, all the time, while working with female clients.

The third aspect of equality is in the sessions themselves, where the counsellor is treating the client as an equal adult most of the time. (When she is 'parenting' (see Chapter 2) this is done as part of the session, not the whole of it. At the end there is always some adult-to-adult exchange.)

The First Session

For most of us, putting the client at ease, perhaps offering them a cup of tea, or talking about their journey is more important at the very beginning than anything else. Clients usually need to feel nurtured. Only then do we talk to them about the counselling process and begin 'interviewing' them. We would usually ask them if they minded us taking notes.

The skills needed for the initial interview are basically social skills for putting a person at ease. Women are generally especially familiar with these skills in their traditional roles as hostesses, although, being seen mainly as *female skills*, they have been devalued by society. In any constructive human interaction, the development of safety and trust, really listening and respecting the other, are vital. They must be established as the underlying basis of the relationship before moving on. We could see this in terms of 'mothering' and 'fathering' qualities. In any encounter, we usually need to go through the 'mother stage' first. Meetings and other encounters that jump straight to the 'father stage' of 'getting down to business' can create unnecessary feelings of aggression and frustration. In counselling, many clients report that they felt furious with therapists or counsellors who did not make them feel at ease. Some strict Freudians say nothing at the beginning, believing that the way clients deal with this helps to uncover their unconscious patterns, but to me this is simply rude, and detracts from the sense of equality that we are trying to build up. There is usually ample opportunity later on to explore unconscious patterns.

What expectations does the client have of counselling itself? Has she had any previous experience or has she read about it? Clients range from the very 'therapeutically sophisticated' to those who know nothing at all. The more sophisticated come to the first session knowing that they are not there to be 'cured' by a counsellor. They know that they have to do the work, and that it is ultimately up to them to be open to change and growth. The counsellor is there as a guide rather than as a dictator. But for others who are more familiar with the medical model of authoritative cure, this approach has to be spelled out. This can be done verbally at the beginning, or on a leaflet or handout that is sent or given to them at the start. Counselling should be 'demystified' and clients given as much information about the process as possible at the beginning, and when appropriate, later on too. This also helps to equalize the relationship, for information is power.

Today there is a bewildering array of different therapies or counselling organizations and techniques on offer, and it is a good idea to start by giving some general information about the whole field to prospective clients at the beginning of their first session. This will also include describing how our own approach differs from others and what its limits are, as well as its strengths. As feminist counsellors vary in the techniques they use, some may be more body-orientated, while others only use talking. For some people, at a certain stage of their lives, body work might be more appropriate than talking on its own, so the first session should involve assessing the client's particular needs. We might conclude that they would be better off seeing another counsellor or that there might be groups such as consciousness-raising groups that they could attend in addition to the counselling, and would therefore discuss these options with them. At different stages of our lives we need different kinds of counselling. For example, a woman dealing with painful feelings of rage and love towards her father may find it useful to work with a male counsellor, while a woman just emerging from a humiliating marriage might need to work with a feminist counsellor *and* attend a consciousness-raising group.

Practical Issues

Once the client has been given basic information about the counselling, she should be told about practical issues, such as payment. Most feminist counsellors operate a sliding scale of charges because we realize that economic hierarchies affect us all and we want to be available for those on low incomes. We should explain when and how we expect to be paid, and settle whether the client wants to come for a certain period or on an open-ended basis, and whether fortnightly or weekly, for example. We also have to be totally clear with our clients about boundaries. For example, if we work in fifty-minute sessions, we need to stick to that timing, while trying to let each session draw to a natural end. The counsellor and client should not socialize outside the sessions, as this would confuse the roles. Counselling should be seen as special, separate from the rest of the client's life. Some clients have great difficulty in understanding and keeping to boundaries, and so it is vital for the counsellor to maintain her own clarity about them, and stick to them, having explained the 'rules' at the start.

At the beginning the client may well have questions about the counselling or the counsellor. Feminist counsellors try to answer such questions as honestly as possible. How far 'personal' questions are fully answered is a matter for the counsellor to decide about beforehand; the boundary between the role of counsellor and that of friend needs to be maintained.

Having established a rapport and set the scene for the client, if she wishes to continue you will need some information about her. Counsellors vary as to how much information they ask for at this stage, but there are some essentials, such as name, address, telephone number, age, occupation, medication (if any), doctor, and a description of family background. Then it is appropriate to ask about the problem that has brought them into counselling, but some clients do not feel comfortable starting off by talking about 'the problem', and you may need to approach the subject very gradually, or be satisfied initially with a very general idea of the problem. Most clients will need initially to find in the counsellor a totally accepting and reassuring presence — and this phase or element in counselling is the subject of the next chapter.

3 Getting Started and Building Trust: the 'Mothering' Phase

> All wandering is from the Mother, to the Mother, in the Mother. The movement is in space and space is a receptacle, a vessel, a matrix — as it were the mother or nurse of all becoming.
>
> (Hall, 1980: 36)

In this chapter the word 'mother' is used in a symbolic sense to represent unconditional acceptance and containment.

The devaluing of mothering and of the 'feminine' side of life has resulted in millions of 'unmothered' children even from wealthy and 'successful' backgrounds. Their actual mothers themselves are brought up to believe that the only really valuable achievements are those of the male world. And some women believe this so deeply that they are unable to relax into actual motherhood, with or without careers. The question is not so much 'Should a woman have a career or children?', but 'Why should having and mothering children be such a devalued task?' It is important to note that men are just as capable of 'mothering' as women.

Many adults coming into counselling have not really been mothered in the full sense of the word. This is not their biological mother's fault; rather the blame needs to be laid at the foot of the whole patriarchal society that makes women feel so inadequate and deprives them of a deep sense of pride in their mothering powers. Many women sense this loss and may even feel a double inadequacy. Not only are they not valued in masculine terms, but they don't even feel any 'good' at mothering. This seems to be especially common among highly intellectual women who have somehow lived only on a mental level, out of touch with the physical feelings in the body. They have internalized the patriarchal fear of, as well as fascination with, female bodies.

So many mothers are affected by patriarchal values that they cannot totally accept their own children. Rather they impose on them their own desires for what they would like them to be. Perhaps a mother who left school early will push her own daughter to succeed academically. Her own frustrated urges are projected on to the child who is not allowed just to be herself. Yet her own rage at not being treated equally to men can also be poured on to her children, willing them to 'fail' just as she did, but only in a hidden side of her psyche. The negative desires and envies born of thousands of years of second-class status are rarely conscious.

Mothering is more a state of being and a particular kind of relationship to another, than a fixed personal identity. Unlike the ancient matriarchal religions, modern society has no powerful image of a great mother or indeed of any strong female symbol. The ancient Greek myth of the mother goddess Demeter searching the world for her lost daughter Persephone needs to be rewritten today. Demeter had lost Persephone at the dawning of the patriarchal era, when young women were 'lost' to the male world. Today the daughters are searching the world for their lost 'mother'.

Figure 3   *The lost great mother*

The body in general has been seen as inferior to the mind, and associated with nature and with women. While despising the female body, the children of the patriarchy like to forget that they were all born out of a woman's body. The creation myth of Adam being formed by a male god and Eve being merely an afterthought to keep him company is most revealing of our culture's attitudes. One important aspect of counselling is enabling a client to journey back to where she came from, to her own 'natural' body, to animal beginnings, to the mother's womb. She may need to rediscover the lost child within her. She may even need to rediscover her own body that she has deliberately 'lost' as something to be despised unless it happens to fit in with the particular male fantasies of the time and be the 'right' shape.

For this process to be allowed to happen the counsellor, whether male or female, needs to play the role of accepting mother, comfortable in her or his own body, solid, present, simply being there.

The First Session with Julia

The woman we call Julia is 29 years old. She arrives for her first session looking confident and dressed in comfortable, casual but fashionable clothes. She is dark-haired and dark-skinned, with piercing eyes and an anxious smile. She is quite thin and sits down rather awkwardly on the sofa. I ask her about her journey and we exchange some comments on cycling in the city. After a general introduction as outlined in Chapter 2, I begin by asking her some questions, such as why does she want counselling? She answers these thoroughly and in considerable detail, while perched on the edge of her seat, leaning towards me, her eyes fixed anxiously on mine. She seems eager to please. She says she wants counselling because she 'sometimes feels panicky' and 'seems to have no aim in life'.

She tells me that her parents are both university professors and had very high hopes for her own academic achievement, but now that she has obtained her PhD, she feels that she doesn't want to continue doing research. For nearly two years she has been doing voluntary work for a women's centre. She is the oldest of a family of three. She feels that she is closer to her father than her mother. Julia says that her parents were very liberal and didn't try to push her at school, but she felt the pressure anyway. It seems that they were two very busy people and didn't spend much time with their children, but when they did they would rarely stop the children doing what they wanted. Julia felt that her mother wasn't strict enough with the two younger children; sometimes she had herself had to act like a mother to them. She talked somewhat disparagingly about her mother but made it clear that she deeply admired her father.

Her relationships with men have not been satisfactory, she thinks, because they are jealous of her success and can't cope with her winning arguments. She also says that she feels very unconfident and occasionally gets panic attacks when going into stressful situations, such as parties.

At this stage, as a counsellor, I am getting first impressions of Julia as a person. All those clues mentioned in the last chapter are absorbed, such as her clothes and accent that gave a superficial impression of confidence. But I am also getting an intuitive feel for the vibrations or energy patterns of the person 'behind' the spoken words and surface appearance. I am aware of Julia's anxiety and eagerness to please and her apparent discomfort at being in her own body. As yet I have not made detailed guesses as to her underlying patterns and problems, but I sense that she is not totally happy with her 'femaleness', and notice much suppressed rage underneath her placatory manner.

In addition to getting information from her, I am also giving her a sense that I do understand her. I feed back what she tells me about having to play the mother role by suggesting that it must have been hard. She does then show a brief glimpse of the anger underneath: 'Mother would have let them get away with murder.' It seems as though she is unconsciously asking me to be a different kind of mother for her. I am to be the mother who is totally focused on her, the mother who does not give special indulgent attention to younger brothers, but also the mother who is 'strict' and has boundaries. I realize that I will have to provide some remothering of a much more containing nature than the mothering she had in real life. She appears to long for the kind of unconditional acceptance that may rarely have existed in such a high-achieving and intellectual family.

The First Session with Mary

The second client we will call Mary. She is 24. She arrives early for the first appointment, dressed in rather scruffy, hippy-style clothes. Mary has long brown hair and a sad, pale face. She sits hunched up on the sofa looking at the floor. After telling me about her job as a nanny and about her husband who works in a health-food shop, she goes quiet. Mary clearly does not find it easy to talk. She often stops in the middle of a sentence. I allow plenty of silences and she does eventually tell me that her parents are shopkeepers and strict Catholics. She did not do well at school and has always felt stupid.

Mary is the youngest of a family of five and was treated as the baby for as long as she could remember. She had escaped family pressures to be a good little Catholic girl by running away with her boyfriend Jim when she was 16. They lived in squats in London for a while before joining a housing association. Mary had always worked with children, while Jim had had a series of odd jobs and was often unemployed. They lived communally with six other people, but Mary felt that she did more than her fair share of the work. She gave me the impression that life was hard and that she was used to playing the role of victim. Jim was clearly the dominant one of the pair. They now had a child, James, aged three. Being 'alternative' sort of people, they tried to share the child-care arrangements, but Mary thought that she still took the major responsibility.

Mary had come to counselling because she was not sleeping well and was depressed. Her homeopathic healer had suggested that counselling would be a good complement to the alternative medicine that she was also using. In this first interview I took down details of the medicines she was using and the name and phone number of her homeopathic healer.

It seemed at first that Mary's problem was almost the opposite to that of Julia. She seemed to have been 'mothered', or rather 'smothered', too much. She had never been given the chance to be her own person, having gone straight from what sounded like a restrictive family environment to a somewhat oppressive relationship within a communal environment. I guessed from the way she kept stopping and looking down that she was not used to being properly listened to or taken seriously. So it seemed that to begin with, the kind of mothering that Mary needed was to be properly listened to. Just by focusing completely on her and by resisting the temptation to jump in and rescue her, during silences, I felt I could help her feel more confident. But she was so used to 'playing' the victim role, unconsciously, that I expected her to try to put me in the 'persecutor' role of 'forcing her to do or be what I wanted her to be'. It would probably take a while for Mary to build up enough trust in me to begin to let go of her victim patterns and express her own needs assertively.

For many women, coming into counselling can be the first time they have been properly listened to. In everyday conversation women tend to be interrupted a lot by men wanting to put their points across. What women have to say is often valued less than what men have to say, simply because women are valued less in general. Most children of either sex are not taken seriously and are frequently humiliated, e.g. by being laughed at when they are serious, or by being patronized. But little boys can later identify with the powerful male hierarchy and get their own back by patronizing women and girls in their turn. One hierarchy, such as adults over children, is linked to another, such as males over females. The repressed rage of humiliated children easily spills over into sadism and the persecution of those thought to be weaker. And while men often internalize the persecutor role, women like Mary internalize the victim role. And if, like Mary, they have also had strict and repressive parents, the fear of confrontation and standing up for themselves is almost overwhelming. The fear of being physically or even psychologically attacked may even be based on actual or threatened incidents in their childhoods. Mary could not remember much of her childhood, but thought that it had been fairly happy. I suspected that there might be some painful memories lurking in the unconscious, but it would take time to get to them.

Like Julia, Mary's main objective for counselling was to become more confident and understand herself better. But she experienced depression that she wanted to 'get rid of'. Both these clients had enough knowledge of therapy and counselling to know that I was not going to behave like a doctor and cure them of their problems, but I still sensed a glimmer of that hope in Mary's pleading eyes. Yet she was very knowledgeable about alternative medicine and believed in self-help and in the wisdom of the body to heal itself. She knew that she was supposed to do all the work, but . . . . With Julia, it seemed that she was prepared to do whatever I thought she was supposed to do in counselling. So long as she was pleasing me, she was willing to do anything. Mary was rather more wary and even implied that she wasn't sure that counselling could help at all. A part of Mary was almost setting herself up to 'fail' even before she had started, which had apparently been the pattern all her life. And the hierarchies of the family and, even more oppressively the school system which had early on 'labelled' her as 'slow', had ensured that she remained comfortably and safely, but miserably, at the bottom.

The First Session with Louise

The third client, Louise, 38, arrived exactly on time, dressed quite elegantly and wearing heavy make-up. She sat down firmly and grinned brightly. She was well-built, with carefully combed black hair. She had come mainly because of an eating problem that Weight Watchers hadn't helped. A friend had suggested that she tried counselling. Louise said she didn't know much about it, didn't know what to expect, but was willing to give it a try.

It turned out that she was also not getting on too well with her husband at the moment. Louise was very forthcoming about her family and her past. Her father had been a builder, but he had left home when she was 13. Her mother had had quite a struggle bringing up Louise and her sister Susan on her own. Susan was apparently two years younger than Louise; they never got on very well and it seems there was still a lot of jealousy. Louise felt that Susan was her mother's favourite, while she was the one who was always criticized. She felt that her mother had never praised or encouraged her.

Louise works in the housing department of the local council. She used to work part-time, when her sons, aged 13 and 15, were younger, but now she works full-time and has recently been promoted. She is really fed up with being overweight and hates herself for her lack of control over food. She has a pattern of dieting and then bingeing.

At first Louise does seem to be looking to me for some advice on eating. 'Do I know of a really good diet?' I spend some time in this first session explaining to her what counselling is about and that I am not there to cure her, but that together we will explore what is going on underneath. Why is she bingeing? What is going on emotionally for her? Perhaps there are sides of herself that she doesn't know about or doesn't like very much that we need to get to know better. I am not going to judge her and give her any more high standards that she is supposed to live up to. I get the impression that she has spent much of her life trying to live up to impossibly high standards.

Louise talks a lot in the session, hardly giving me a chance to get a word in edgeways. It feels as though she is desperately trying to control the situation. Her fear may be that if she isn't totally in control, then chaos will result and all hell will break loose. But I do feed back enough of what she says to show considerable understanding of her problems, and towards the end she begins to talk about her husband and how he always tries to put her down. Yet at the same time she is expected to have meals cooked and the house tidy even though she also works full-time. However, she adds that he is hopeless at cooking and housework, so she would rather do it really. I sense a familiar ambivalence between (1) liking the power of being in control at home, and (2) resenting the responsibility at the same time. Before leaving, Louise says that it has been a great relief to talk so openly about her dissatisfactions.

For Louise it seemed vital that I was 'on her side'. The way she talked about her relationship with her mother in that first session revealed a sense that her mother had never been fair. She had criticized Louise a lot and, in Louise's eyes at least, she had given the younger sister preferential treatment throughout most of their childhood. Somehow it felt as though whatever Louise did, it would never be good enough for her mother. All her life she had been trying to live up to some imaginary standard that her mother had set.

Louise's mother too had been deeply affected by the social hierarchies of our society. She was born to a large poor family in the East End of London, but had moved out when she married and had tried desperately to 'improve' herself. Apparently the two girls were always beautifully dressed, without a speck of dirt to be seen on their clothes. The house was always tidy and the children weren't allowed to enter the 'parlour' except on Sundays. The mother sounded almost obsessive about cleanliness. Somehow being clean represented a 'higher' rung on the hierarchical social ladder. Her great fear was of sinking 'down' to the 'dirty' depths of the 'lower classes'. This seemed to have transferred itself unconsciously into Louise's mind as a sense of basic inferiority. The message was, 'You are only acceptable if you look good on the surface, if you are clean and neat.' I was reminded here of all those washing-powder advertisements with smiling mothers gazing adoringly at pure white T-shirts just extracted from brand new washing machines. There was, and still is, enormous pressure on women to have 'high' standards of cleanliness and tidiness. While there may once have been health reasons for being scrupulously clean, today the symbolic meanings of cleanliness seem to play a much bigger part. It has become associated with acceptability, while dirt, untidiness and mess has been associated with unacceptability. Dirt is also associated with the body, with nature and even with being female. A menstruating woman is still unconsciously thought of in the biblical way as 'unclean' by many people.

The housewifely obsession with cleanliness is the result of both class and gender hierarchies. For Louise's mother, all her energies were geared towards moving 'up' in the world. And no doubt little children or babies who make a lot of mess were not exactly part of her plan! But again, it is not helpful to blame the mother. She was herself a victim of the class system and society's obsession with upward mobility. The contradictions of the society are internalized within its individual members. Louise's feelings of inadequacy, coupled with very high expectations and standards of perfection, are not unusual today.

Louise showed a fear of criticism by looking at me anxiously every time she said something negative. At first it feels important to show a basic acceptance of her, with no judgements at all. She has been so used to judgements and working out what she should or shouldn't be doing, thinking, feeling or looking like, that it was important for me not to add to her lists with more do's and don'ts. Louise would often ask me 'Do you think I should ask my husband to do the washing up, diet, stop dieting, etc.?', and it was quite hard to refuse each time to make any judgements. It was even hard just to listen in a non-judgemental way, because of the way she kept looking at me for a reference.

It was also clear from this first session that her values were quite different from mine in many respects. She still had what I perceive as stereotyped ideas about a wife's role in marriage. She also seemed to be strongly materialistic, but I did like and respect the spirit underneath all the social assumptions and expectations. I thought of her as a lively being who had been fossilized through fear into a shape that didn't quite fit. But it was the being, not the shape, that I was relating to. While I heard what she was saying to me and accepted it, I did not agree with many of her statements. In time perhaps some of these could be questioned gently in the sessions, but to do so now would simply repeat the pattern of her own actual mothering. I would be invalidating her reality, and criticizing her. Her mother seemed to have invalidated her own female, working-class realities in order to appear acceptable to the masculine, patriarchal realities of society. With Louise we needed to get back in touch with her own reality, her own body, her own background, her own being. So the kind of re-mothering she seemed to need was a non-critical, validating kind. She needed to be taken seriously and accepted.

The sense that 'I am on your side' is very important in feminist counselling. Most children, boys as well as girls, grow up feeling that the grown-ups are not 'on their side'. The child's reality is not taken seriously. Children are treated so often as if they were the 'enemy' who have to be kept under control all the time. Perhaps there is also the fear of the child side within ourselves, that dirty, messy, unacceptable side so many of us adults are anxious to destroy. Children still tend to see parents, teachers and other authority figures as 'the enemy' because children pick up adults' attitudes. Even adults coming into counselling, especially if they are from a lower class than the counsellor, sometimes see her as 'the enemy'. Somehow the counsellor is on the other side. In patriarchal society everything and everybody is divided into opposing 'sides' and usually some kind of power-struggle is expected between them, resulting in a winner and a loser. So deeply is this model ingrained in our heads, that many counselling relationships also become a struggle for power and control. But in feminist counselling we work with a different model. There are no opposing sides, in unconscious battle with each other. We may have our differences, our opposite roles, such as counsellor and client, but we are symbolically dancing with these opposites, weaving them into a pattern that will help the clients understand themselves better and express all the previously opposing sides within themselves.

Different Kinds of Mothering

This first stage of counselling can last for weeks or even years, depending on the particular client. The general symbolic concept of mothering is important during this stage, but different styles of 'mothering' are appropriate for different clients.

1   *Holding.* One aspect of mothering is holding and containing the whole client, including everything that they say or do in the sessions. It is like being a vessel or cooking-pot that has strong sides and contains all the elements as they move and change within it. The

counsellor provides a safe and stable environment for the client to be in. Simply being there in the same place at the same time each week is a form of holding. The counsellor's attention focused on the client all the time also provides holding. She does not lose interest or let her attention wander when the client talks too much or too little. She may react when it's appropriate, but she is also simply a presence, another person being with the client through whatever ups and downs she is experiencing. Sometimes, for example, when a client is crying, it may be appropriate for the counsellor literally to hold her or at least put a hand out to touch her.

2 *Letting go.* The counsellor can also provide a space where the client can learn to be herself, to listen to what she really feels, as opposed to being and feeling what others have told her she should feel. The counsellor does not have expectations of her. The counsellor does not advise her. There is also a sense of separateness that may not have existed with the client's real mother. The counsellor does not mind what the client does; it does not reflect on her. She does not have a vested interest in the client's achievements. She can let the client be.

3 *Non-judgemental Acceptance.* The counsellor does not judge the client. Whatever she says or does is accepted. The counsellor genuinely believes that she is OK and conveys this feeling implicitly or even explicitly by saying things like 'It's OK to feel angry', or 'You have a right to feel what you feel.'

Julia needed very basic, almost physical 'holding' to help her feel secure in her body and in her being. Mary needed the kind of mothering that could 'let her go', that trusted her to be herself. She especially needed to be listened to. Louise needed to be accepted as she is, not judged or criticized as she was by her real mother, who had been so affected by patriarchal attitudes.

All of us, even as adults, need all these forms of 'mothering'. And all of us are potentially capable of providing all three aspects of 'mothering', men as well as women. But at different times of our lives we need more of one form than another. In fact we may need some 'mothering' before we can go on to develop any new stage of growth, whether this be moving from childhood into adolescence, from being single to being married, or from one career to another. It seems to provide a kind of grounding, an unconditional acceptance, of our very existence.

The Mother as Symbol

Symbolically, our relation to what Jungians would call the 'mother' archetype is what grounds us in material reality and in the essential spirit of our being. When this relationship is distorted we have little sense of fully 'being here'. We may even feel that we do not really have the right to exist. We cannot accept ourselves as we are; only in terms of achievement and acceptability to the patriarchal culture. And modern society has a deeply damaged relationship to the 'mother' archetype. Although this helps create the low status and insecurity that actual biological mothers and carers feel, it is also a deeper psychological problem for our entire age. An archetype is an image that represents important human needs, fears, desires and dreams. The mother is an important image. We need to recognize its symbolic nature and separate that from the live complex human beings who give birth to children.

We live in a deeply symbolic society. We fall in love with symbols; we relate to each other through symbols. Many therapists today prefer to talk about parenting, or about unconditional positive regard, in which the therapist is seen as re-parenting the client, through unconditional acceptance. These words do not have quite the same numinous symbolic power as does the word 'mother', but we can be on dangerous territory if we use the term 'mothering' without stressing the differences between the symbolic meaning of the word and actual human beings who have the label 'mother'. It is also vital to talk about the 'mother*ing*', as it is essentially a function, not a thing, not static. It is one aspect of all human relationships. It is a particular kind of relating, one that is generally undervalued in our society. It can be a part of any relationship between friends, lovers, work colleagues, as well as between parents and children.

Many clients come into counselling looking for mothers. They may have a particular image in mind, or they may project their desire on to any figure, male or female, who happens to be sitting in the counsellor's chair. Some human beings fit the symbolic image or archetype of the mother more easily than others. For example, the large and maybe older female is likely to fit our physical image of 'mother' more easily than a thin young man. But even if the physical realities of the counselling situation do not reflect the client's experience of her real mother, it is likely that she will make the connections. After experience of a rejecting mother, Louise probably expected unconsciously that I too would reject her, so she finished the session looking at her watch, and getting up. She did not want to give me a chance to reject her by telling her that time was up, as she expected a 'mother' to.

One client actually told me that I reminded her of her mother, while another said I was not a bit like her mother, but still the second client responded to me as she did to her own mother in many ways, i.e. very defensively. The whole counselling situation is set up to recreate a 'mother-child' interaction and the particular patterns that the client had with her real mother or other close carer usually emerge sooner or later. It may be that the counsellor is seen at first as all-powerful, all-knowing, or even 'a perfect mother'. For some of my clients this image remained strong even when they knew 'intellectually' that I was not all-knowing, and was certainly not perfect. It often takes an incident, when, for example, I make an irrelevant comment, miss the point, or even simply go away on holiday, to give the client real awareness of my non-perfection. For one woman it took nearly two years, for another over a year, before she could see me as a human being with both strengths and weaknesses. She had a dream in which I was being criticized by two other knowledgeable women and my client was sticking up for me against them. This dream marked a deep change in the client's life and it was important that she could see me as neither high 'up' on a distant pedestal, or 'down' there being a totally useless counsellor criticized by everyone, but she was still able to value me, as she was now also valuing herself more.

The Totally 'Good' or 'Bad' Mother

Many clients come with the idea of the opposites of 'perfect' mother and 'bad' mother etched deeply into their unconscious. I might become the perfect mother for them while they talk of their real mother as absolutely awful. Julia had this approach at the beginning of our work together. I was the good mother and her own mother was all bad. For some clients it can be quite a breakthrough to criticize their own mothers. And while they are doing that, they need a 'good' mother to keep the balance. Both Julia and Louise saw me as the 'Good Mother' at first. But Mary was unable to be critical of her own real mother at all. So I was seen as the 'bad' mother to begin with. She had given up hope of finding the perfect nurturing mother, while Julia and Louise both still hoped for such mothering perfection.

They were, however, all three affected by the 'mother' archetype in our society that only allows for a one-sided 'good' mother, and hides away the possibility of the other side, of the 'bad' or destructive, frightening mother. Instead we have fairy stories full of 'evil' witches to carry the negative side. Mothers, like other symbolic people, are supposed to be either 'good' or 'bad', never both. We have few images that include the so-called negative as well as the so-called positive sides of mother. Yet it seems to be vital for 'healthy' growth that we accept the rhythmic ambivalence of life, the way that everything is not clear-cut good or bad. And this understanding needs to start with parents and especially mothers. If we see our mother as totally good, then all the 'badness' that we sense is still around must be ours. So we think of ourselves as totally bad instead. The thought of mother being bad is much too threatening. After all, at first we depend on her for our very life.

For little girls, especially, this link with mother is particularly intense. Together they make up a whole, one side good and the other side bad. The real mother may even project her unacceptable side on to the daughter. Clients often come into counselling quite scared of finding out that their mothers were not 'perfect' or at least not 'all good'. Some say that they feel disloyal as soon as any negative remarks about their mothers come up. Others will be so defensive at first that they even say 'My mother was great, I don't want to look at my relationship with her at all.'

A few clients come feeling nothing but negative feelings towards their mothers. One young Irish client I had painted her mother as a real monster who treated her daughter rather like a household slave. It was only after some weeks of counselling that she found anything 'good' to say about her mother. And she also began to look at reasons for her mother's cruel behaviour. Often there seems to be unconscious competition between mothers and daughters. One client told me that her mother had dragged her to the hairdresser every month to cut her hair short like a boy's. There seemed to be a great fear and jealousy connected with the daughter's sexuality. The client had repressed most of the deep rage she felt towards her mother about this cruelty. Allowing themselves to experience rage helps many of these clients feel better about themselves. They can take back some of the 'goodness' that used to be invested in the mother. Eventually they can usually see that the mother is both 'good' and 'bad' and so are they.

The counsellor too will eventually be seen as both 'good' and 'bad', but it is likely that at first she will be mainly seen as one or the other. It is important that she recognizes these projections and is personally detached from any of her own anxieties about being a 'good' or 'bad' counsellor, mother or person. Often clients need to have a 'good' mother image of the counsellor for the sessions to work at all. If the projection is all bad, the client may not return. There may be a stage later when the counsellor is seen as the 'bad mother', once trust has been built up, when the feelings involved can be usefully explored.

Although most 'good' or 'bad' labels are clients' projections, there are also objective realities that may be in the background. Some client/counsellor mixtures will not work for reasons that probably have more to do with personality, 'chemistry', or background, politics etc. than the intrinsic or projected 'goodness' or 'badness' of either of them, and where this is the case the only thing to do is to stop the counselling.

Valuing the Defences

In the mothering phase the clients' defences are accepted and used, while in later phases they may be confronted more directly.

Even though the counsellor usually recognizes projections and other defences right at the beginning of counselling, she does not have immediately to start 'battering them down'. Feminist counsellors recognize that people have grown up in a world where they are 'taught' that everyone and everything is either good or bad. They have been brought up in a world that humiliates little children and insists on preserving social hierarchies at the expense of authentic self-expression. We have all had to build up defences in order to survive in such a world, and we need to respect those defences. We need to work with and through the defences, not to attack them with a 'masculine' aggressive approach. This does not mean that feminist counsellors collude with clients in preserving their defences throughout counselling: there are times when confrontation is appropriate. But during this first stage especially we would use a different model from one involving attack and 'breaking' down, which is so common in many other approaches to counselling. We would use the model of rhythm again. The defences are rigid ways of reacting, such as always seeing authority figures as 'bad' and running away from them. In counselling we are aiming to loosen up those reactions and help them to be more flexible. It might still sometimes be appropriate to 'run away' from particular authority figures, but not from all of them. Defensive responses can be respected while at the same time we hope to melt them down.

For example, Julia was clearly very defensive about her body. Her fear of disapproval had frozen her energies, so that her whole body was stiff and awkward. Her neck and shoulders were especially stiff, as she was so busy unconsciously keeping her head apart from other parts of her body. Her defences included her rationalization of everything that happened to her. She was keeping her 'head' firmly in control. Everything could be explained away through verbal reason, so that she wouldn't have to face messy, painful feelings that threatened to emerge. Yet Julia had been very successful with her defences and her clear articulation of problems was admirable. While listening to her, I thought, 'This is partly a big defence', but I recognized that it was also valuable in its own right. It wasn't just a defence; it was both a defence and an objectively useful way of understanding.

At first I related to Julia on the verbal, reasonable level that she was used to. I showed that I understood what she was telling me. I shared a few 'insights' in the first and second sessions that could be appreciated on a purely intellectual level. But by the third session I was able to be with her silently and encourage her to stay with her immediate feelings. Instead of battering the defences it is often enough just to bring the client gently back to the here and now. How was she feeling at present, with me in this room? She lived so much in her 'head' that at first she was hardly 'here' at all. Noticing what her body was doing was also important in bringing her back into the here and now. This included paying attention to the way she was sitting. Quite quickly she began noticing these things for herself. But that too was partly a defence against me pointing them out to her, which she construed as criticism. As we related on an adult-to-adult level as well, we were able to laugh together about the defences we noticed.

At first laughter was a useful way of discharging pent-up feelings and building a sharing relationship. Later on it was important to stop and be serious. After about four sessions I was able to point out how often she smiled or giggled when talking about sad and painful events. The smiling was of course another defence, but this could not have been pointed out so effectively in the first session. She would have been too embarrassed. By the sixth session I was able to ask her to repeat statements that were painful without smiling or laughing.

With one client, a man, who had been coming to see me for two months, I simply said one day, 'Can you just *be* for a while?' He too had used living in the 'head' as a safety mechanism for not feeling anything. He was very 'frozen'. Those few moments of 'being' in the room with me had a profound effect on his defences. It began a long process of melting, during which he actually returned to his own body and began to be himself. But he had to be ready himself for such a change. He also needed to feel that the sessions with me were safe 'places' where he was being 'held' in a way he never had been by his own mother. The ability to trust one's own being can only develop within the safety of strong, accepting and containing 'mothering'.

Mary's defences included her own inarticulateness and dependency on others to take the lead. She was so used to being interrupted in conversations that she would give up easily. Her sentences would trail off. For her, melting the defences meant encouraging her to finish sentences. This meant that she had to be really committed to what she was saying, for the confusion and silence often hid strong feelings and opinions that she was actually scared to acknowledge and articulate.

It was also vital to allow long silences and space for her to fill. The refusal to jump in and rescue was my way of melting her defences. Attacking her verbally would have forced her back even further into her shell.

However, she needed a great deal of positive feedback when she did talk. She was 'rewarded' for expressing clearly her thoughts and feelings. In the same way 'good' mothers reward their child's attempts to talk, walk, feed themselves, etc. If the mother is always jumping in and doing it for them, the child becomes discouraged and may even, like Mary, give up. Mary, as the youngest in the family, had 'carried' all the fears the others had about 'failing' or not coping. The mother had kept her own sense of competence and control partly by projecting her own inadequacies on to Mary. In a sense Mary's incompetence and low self-esteem was the hidden opposite of her own mother. Sometimes when people like Mary reconnect with their own strong, competent side, their mothers suddenly find that they cannot cope any more. Their coping has depended on the daughter *not* coping. The same pattern can even be seen in friendships where one person 'plays' mother and the other is the 'weaker' child. Eventually counselling aims to help people express both sides, the 'strong' and 'vulnerable' sides that we all have.

Louise's non-stop talking seemed a more difficult defence to melt and work with. Any directions or interruptions were experienced as criticism and she would visibly crumple. This made it difficult to 'be' in the here and now. It seemed that this first stage of 'mothering' with Louise would have to concentrate on understanding her childhood and where her present problems came from. We would be like two detectives, working together to discover clues as to why she was having difficulties in her life. After four weeks Louise did acknowledge that she still really longed for her mother's approval. Again, as with Mary, she had been carrying the unacceptable sides of her mother, the 'not good enough' side. In fact her mother had never felt 'good enough'. Louise would need to experience and express an enormous amount of rage towards her mother before she could see her as both 'good' and 'bad', herself a victim of cruel social hierarchies. While seeing her mother as 'all bad' for a while, it was important that I remained the 'good' mother. Only after this stage would we be able to explore the 'bad' side of me and counselling, and the ambivalence of 'being'.

Throughout this stage and for the whole process of counselling, I am always aware that the real mothers our clients talk about were themselves given an impossible role. It is hardly surprising that most of us did not get the mothers that we needed. We did not have mothers who were comfortable with all sides of themselves, who were assertive and confident and, at the same time as demanding space for themselves, gave us space to be ourselves. Often we did not have clear boundaries between ourselves and our mothers, or between our needs and those of others. In these fifty-minute sessions counsellors, male or female, are trying to provide a different, more balanced, kind of mothering; a mothering with boundaries.

4 Identifying Themes: Separating out the Opposites

Joy and Woe are woven fine,
A clothing for the Soul divine,
Under every grief and pine
Runs a joy with silken twine.
(William Blake, 'Auguries of Innocence')

The second stage of counselling involves identifying patterns in the client's behaviour and thinking, or themes that seem to run through all that she is saying. This stage might begin in the very first session or it may take several weeks to develop. It does not follow in a linear fashion from the first stage of 'mothering'; rather it is contained within the first stage, grows out of it but remains within it. This apparent paradox may be hard to understand as we all tend to think in a linear, uni-directional way, and clients coming to counselling also expect a one-way movement from stage to stage, whereas, as we have seen before, change in a *spiral* way is more helpful. The whole process can be seen as contained within the transforming vessel or container of the 'mother' of the counselling environment (see Figure 4).

While the first stage is simply distinguished by the counsellor offering containment and unconditional acceptance, the second stage involves focusing on specific issues. It involves concentrating on some areas of discourse rather than others. It involves creating priorities. It does not mean that everything the client says is not accepted; it just means that the counsellor brings certain recurring themes to the client's attention.

It is also the stage at which the client herself defines her own goals and thinks about what she hopes to get out of counselling. Sometimes it helps actually to write down some of these goals. They range from the general to the very specific. Examples include 'I want to be more confident'; 'I want to stop being fat.' Some of these goals might be inappropriate for the kind of counselling on offer. For example, when clients say that they want to lose weight, I usually ask them what this means in terms of their own bad feelings about themselves or about their 'fat' side. I would never personally work with clients solely to help them lose weight or reduce drug-intake. These are symptoms of underlying problems in our society as well as in the

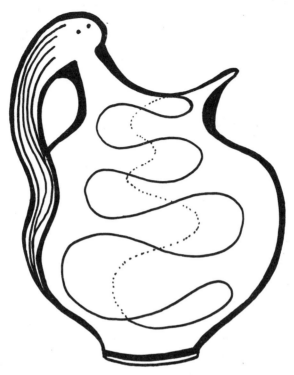

Figure 4   *The counsellor as containing vessel*

client's own life. Helping a woman to lose weight would be colluding with all the social pressures that make her so obsessed with slimming. Rather I would help her to look at those pressures and encourage her to discover her own real needs.

Focusing on the whole person rather than on one behavioural problem seems to be more effective in the long term in this kind of counselling. However, we have all been deeply affected by social pressures, and we need to respect the desires and goals that clients bring to us, as well as helping them to explore the underlying issues. We might look at the need for control that often underlies eating problems, or help them to redefine goals, e.g. from 'losing weight' to 'accepting myself as I am', which one client decided eventually was what she *really* wanted.

Some Common Themes: Conflicting Opposites

All the people I have ever known and worked with have been deeply affected by the hierarchies of society. Inside each person these hierarchies are reproduced. First there always seems to be some kind of split, for example, between mind and body, the 'I' and the 'Not I', the strong side and the weak side, the child and the parent within. Some separation and splitting is necessary for the growing baby in any society to develop a sense of herself, and as a separate being she must split off from her mother, but in modern Western society all separations tend to be dramatic and permanent. The various opposites such as the self and the not-self, child and adult, thinking and feelings, are treated not just as different and interconnected, but as inferior and superior. The superior side is supposed to control or dominate the inferior side. As parents control children, so the internal 'parent conscience' must control the 'childlike' desires. The strong side must control and repress the vulnerable side; the head must rule the heart. This model has permeated patriarchal society, reaching right into its very soul. And this model is the underlying structure responsible for much of our psychological misery. All the complex and varied inner conflicts and unexpressed emotions are connected to the hierarchies of the society into which we are born. Humiliated children turn into oppressive adults. Repressed and frustrated mothers who society treats as second class, repress and frustrate their children. Oppressed workers oppress their wives, and so it goes on.

However feminist counsellors do not 'preach' radical thinking to their clients. Such understanding has to develop within the client. All we do is to help them explore their situation in a way that enables them to develop that understanding. (The way we do this is discussed later in this chapter and described in detail in the next chapter.) Sometimes it is enough to sit there quietly while they do all the analysing. One woman said in her very first session 'I seem to be two different people — a very timid one and a super-confident one.' With another woman I pointed out to her the pattern of opposite behaviours that she was describing to me as a string of separate incidents. Now we explore some particularly common sets of opposites.

The Desire for Intimacy and Fear of Rejection
These opposites commonly recognized in psychology come up again and again in counselling work. The patterns that people use to cope with this particular split do however vary enormously. Some people withdraw from the conflict altogether and even pretend that they don't have the desire. In such cases the fear is overwhelming. With these clients, helping them to express their needs and desires will be a vital part of the counselling. Other clients reject others before they are rejected by them. It is often difficult to work with such clients, as

they frequently reject the counsellor in overt or subtle ways. It is vital for the counsellor not to reject them, and when it feels safe enough, point out to them what they are doing. Often they can identify this pattern for themselves, but some may even leave counselling when their desire for closeness becomes too threatening. Yet other clients will demand the closeness and either become very dependent and childlike or try to please the counsellor by giving her whatever she thinks the counsellor wants.

The basic pattern that the client uses in life is likely to be reproduced in counselling. When appropriate this too can be pointed out to the client. Whatever the pattern is, it is usually based on the conflict between the desire for closeness and the need for separation. But in fact we all need both. In a non-hierarchical society the early separation would be less traumatic, and so the split between the two opposites would be less pronounced. There the desire for closeness and that for separation would be able to flow rhythmically in the course of a day or even an hour. A good example is the child who explores the room, crawling away from the parent, but then from time to time returns to re-experience the equally vital closeness. In our society extreme separation leads to a strong swing towards the opposite, extreme desire for closeness, with all its fears of rejection and even annihilation, or of being 'eaten up by the other'.

Being Totally in Control or in Complete Chaos

Hierarchical thinking leads to a deep sense of one side of ourselves having to be in control of another. This can be seen in social terms in the class system and in imperialism, where white upper-class males are expected to control and rule over the 'chaotic' masses. In the same way our heads are seen as having to control our messy 'inferior' bodies. Women in the West who have for thousands of years been associated with the body and its perceived inferiority, are at particular pains to control that part of themselves that is so despised. Yet for women, the 'looks' of our bodies are the major source of our self-image, even over our very identity. We are often only defined through our bodies. We are taught to despise and control that which we are. For women especially, the general problems society has with problems of control are played out in our relationships to our bodies. The common syndrome of dieting and bingeing is to do with being totally in control and then letting go completely after feeling so deprived. For being in total control does not allow for the bodily or emotional expression of a person's needs. So after the control must come the swing to the extreme opposite. After bingeing women often hate themselves for being so 'out of control'.

Dependence and Independence

This theme relates to the previous one in that being dependent can feel very scary and 'out of control'. But dependence is also very comforting when it feels safe and not suffocating. We all need to depend sometimes and to be independent at other times. In a less hierarchical society both needs could more easily be satisfied, as dependency would not be seen as a weakness and as an inferior state. But because it is associated with inferiority and connected to the world of women, dependency is despised. Women are supposed to be the dependent ones in patriarchal societies. But often it seems that 'deep down' men are actually just as dependent. The difference is that men take their dependent sides to mothers, girlfriends or wives so that they can go out into the 'real' world showing no 'weakness'. Women, on the other hand, are often made to feel that their only power resides in taking care of their dependants. So we play this one-sided role of caretakers a lot of the time. Meanwhile our own deep 'little girl' dependency needs go unmet and are also seen as inferior. While we often do feel dependent on others, such as men, for our security and estimation of self-worth, those 'deeper' needs for emotional support may remain unsatisfied. We may even be afraid of any 'deep' dependency, fearing perhaps that if we depend a little on someone they will swallow us up or reject us. In our either/or patriarchal society we can only conceive of relationships in terms of either being dependent or independent, and people are seen as either the nurturer or the dependent one. It is hard to see people as both at different times. It is this cognitive model of extreme opposites that leads to most of the fears clients bring to counselling.

Power and Powerlessness

These opposites relate to the previous theme. In our society people and groups are split into those with power and those without, and this split is reflected in the economic and political systems under which we live. Feelings of powerlessness take us back to the fears of babyhood when we were very dependent and couldn't control our parents or our own desires and fears. As with the fear of rejection, people use all kinds of patterns to cope with these fears of powerlessness. Some people try to be totally powerful and in control; many children go through a stage of feeling omnipotent or totally powerful in their fantasies. Some adults never let go of this dream. Others try to be powerful most of the time but have such a deep fear of powerlessness that they don't really convince themselves that they have achieved power. Many people in hierarchical society feel that the only way in which they can feel powerful is to have power over other people. They must control others in order to feel OK about themselves. Yet a deep feeling of powerfulness comes from simply really feeling OK in oneself, and being able to have just *some* control and influence over the immediate environment. Being genuinely powerful also means being able to discover and accept the feelings of powerlessness which we all experience at times over things we cannot change, over tragedies and over losses. Often experiencing and accepting powerlessness is a first step towards a healthy reintegration of the opposite (strong and vulnerable) sides of ourselves.

Perfection and Uselessness
This connects with the previous situation, in which people feel that they must be 'on top'; if not, they will be at the 'bottom'. Either we are winners *or* we are losers. So people feel that they must win always at all cost or else ... The struggle for perfection runs throughout Western society, and its effect on the psyches of millions of women and men is devastating. Underneath the proud success lurks the terror of failure, of the abyss. In a less hierarchical society these opposites would not be so split. Rather success and failure would be seen as two sides of the same coin, both part of the human processes of learning and changing. Instead we have the constant gaze upwards, always upwards, towards 'higher' goals, ideals, perfection. This can be expressed in material terms, an area cleverly exploited by the advertising industry, or it might be expressed in striving for the perfect mate, the perfect family, the perfect novel or the perfect soufflé. This uni-directional attitude leaves behind a train of disappointment, dissatisfaction and feelings of inadequacy in its wake. The alternative, feminist model does not denounce achievements, successes, excellence, but does not always 'look up' to these as the only aim of life. For us life is a process in which failure, rest, being, are just as important as success, activity and doing.

Identifying and Understanding Opposites

The process of counselling involves first identifying these kinds of themes. It also involves the discovery of the client's major opposites within the overall theme. For example, if power is an important theme in one person's life, it may be that her major split is between the all-powerful, omnipotent child within her that can 'make' anything happen in her head, and the frightened, vulnerable body of the opposite child within. It is a split between mind and body as well. Another client with the same main theme may experience it more as a split between the opposites of the controlling 'parent' side within her and the 'out of control' desperately needy 'child' side. So the main theme is not always enough to help us analyse the problem. We need to find her particular opposites.

So for many women the early stages of counselling are spent trying to find out what she 'really' wants, what she 'really' feels and what she 'really' needs. Sometimes the superwoman image is the side of her that she presents to the world. She sees it as the acceptable side. But the other 'unacceptable' side is the one with all the hidden needs and desires. This side can feel so starved that it becomes desperately greedy for the satisfaction of those denied needs. This may lead to compulsive eating, as food is an easier and more controllable form of satisfaction than some of the other things a woman might desire, such as love or self-expression. This 'greedy' side needs to be identified first, but then accepted and nurtured in the counselling sessions. But the woman may also be helped by the understanding that this side feels so awful and out of control because society has made it so difficult for women to admit to, let alone express, their needs and demand to have them met. Books and/or consciousness-raising groups could be used to complement the counselling sessions where long discussions about women and society may not be appropriate.

Issues concerning rejection are also problematic for both men and women, but women's fear of it seems to differ from men's in certain respects. Firstly the separation from mother is often of a different quality. The little boy is always seen as fundamentally different from the mother because of his gender. So she has to work out what he needs by asking him and listening to him, while the girl child is more likely to be seen as similar to the mother, who may just assume that she knows what the girl wants. There is less empathy with the boy, but it means that the boy's actual needs get listened to more easily than the girl's. The little girl is experienced by the mother almost as a part of her. There are often few clear-cut boundaries between them. The little boy however is frequently treated as a separate, almost 'alien' being, from early on in life, usually by the time he is weaned. This 'separation' can be very dramatic and painful after that initial symbiotic connection with mother, but then the little boy goes out into the world where despite, and even because of, his separation from mother, his gender gives him a higher status as a male. His feeling of importance compensates for that painful separation.

I don't believe that we can ever underestimate the power of hierarchies on people's self-esteem. Women still experience themselves and are seen as second-class citizens. This may be unconcscious, covered up by 'equal opportunities' and ideologies of equality, but counsellors and therapists everywhere notice with surprise just how low women's self-esteem actually is. Again and again, men's needs are being put first by those same 'confident' women. Women and all those aspects of society associated with them, such as child-rearing and sensitivity, are still devalued. It is not surprising then that women undervalue themselves and are generally far more self-critical than men.

This extremely low self-esteem makes both separation and rejection especially difficult for women. If a woman is rejected she tends firmly to believe that it is because there is something wrong with her. It is always her fault. And as women are taught to define themselves solely in terms of others and how they are seen by those others, a rejection can feel like a rejection of everything that she is. For all she is depends on the approval of others. While a man will also be hurt, he is more likely still to have his basic sense of self left at the end.

Other issues, like striving for perfection, can make men as well as women feel inadequate for not achieving the dreamed-of heights. But for many women the 'perfection' that they strive for is simply the perfection of appearance, defined in men's terms. It is their unconscious or even conscious aim 'to be perfect for HIM'. Men have tended to put women on pedestals, while at the same time not valuing women's real selves. Being on a pedestal is a very lonely and precarious place to be, especially as falling off it can be a *total* rejection: for women, complete annihilation. When not on the pedestal, the 'real self' is experienced as totally worthless.

Julia

For Julia, the second stage of identifying opposites began in the first session, although the 'mothering' of the first stage continued right through counselling. In fact the identification of themes and opposites was easier for her than allowing herself to be just held and accepted. Noticing themes involved her mind, with which she felt more comfortable than with her body. It was important for me not to let mental analysis take over, and to keep coming back to the first stage of simply being in the here and now, allowing silences and even asking from time to time how she was 'feeling now'.

The mind/body split so common in our Western culture was particularly pronounced in Julia. She was able to recognize in the first session that she associated mental achievement with success, perfection and with her father. It was that side of her that she admired. She talked about wanting to achieve academically and was aware that this was to do with pleasing her father. Yet she also felt very inadequate and unable to please him. She would never be good enough for him. Somehow it felt hopeless. Her opposites were very far apart, with dramatic swings between them. Either she felt superior to everyone and like her father, or she felt absolutely hopeless and rejected by him. Life felt like a constantly losing struggle to win his approval.

Julia had internalized the patriarchal attitude of either/or about nearly everything. When this was pointed out to her, it seemed to be quite a relief. She recognized that pattern at once, and turned to me asking what she should do about it. How could she 'win' with me? I put the question back to her and she thought about it for a while. Then she said that she wanted to be more 'in the middle'. She wanted to feel more 'ordinary', neither superior nor inferior. This provided a useful framework and objective for the counselling work. She also recognized that this related to her desire for her father's approval and that maybe one day she wouldn't need that so much and would be better able to accept herself. But this 'self' also did seem to have opposite sides that had been labelled 'superior' and 'inferior'. One side was clearly the more intellectual side that liked to reason and order everything in her head. This was partly a way of protecting herself from the chaotic feelings in the other side that kept threatening to overwhelm her, but it also had its genuine strength.

It was the other side, the body and feeling side that had been associated with inferiority, that needed to be brought out. While the 'top' side needed to be brought down, the 'bottom' side needed to be brought up! It was this side that seemed to be associated with her mother and with the so-called 'feminine' side of life. In fact, after a few sessions we started calling the two sides the 'mother' side and the 'father' side. The mother side was despised, rather like her own mother. Julia had very few female friends, yet she had a pattern of being attracted to rejecting men with whom she would compete intellectually and end up being defeated by. The social reality of most men not liking more intellectual women was shared, but we also recognized that Julia was making it worse for herself because of her own inner conflicts. She admired charismatic men, like her father, but never really felt good enough for them. Often she was so scared of rejection that she wouldn't even show any interest in them. She thought at first that she was afraid of rejection because her mind wasn't good enough, but it turned out that really she was afraid that her body wasn't good enough, attractive enough. This led us on to an exploration of the body, mother side.

It turned out that this side was very frightened and could not trust the outside world. So the 'father' side had to be completely in control. Julia often used to get a stiff neck which showed how hard she tried to keep her head separate from, and in control of, the rest of her body. Yet in that other side there seemed to be a longing to merge with others, mainly boyfriends. Her fear of rejection and difficulty in separating from a mother who she never felt safe with manifested itself in the desire to lose herself completely in 'the other'. So if the 'mother' side was allowed the 'freedom' to express itself it would simply merge into others and disappear. Therefore staying in control really felt like a matter of life and death. Indeed another important set of opposites for Julia turned out to be total control versus total loss of self.

Mary

Mary had always been the baby of the family, which had given her the advantage of not having to be responsible. But it also meant that she wasn't really 'grown up' either. She seemed to be afraid of any comments that sounded like criticism, so moving into the second stage of separating out particular themes was quite difficult. She appeared to prefer staying in the safety of the first stage of containment by the 'mother'. Separating, even in terms of prioritizing themes and finding opposite sides, felt like a threat. She also looked to me to do all the analysing and thinking. It felt so much easier to be led and taken care of by others. Yet it was clear from the first session that she also felt secretly resentful. Mary's angry side seemed to be very deeply buried and quite unacceptable to her.

As she talked to me about her family it emerged that there were never any confrontations. She couldn't remember her parents ever raising their voices to each other. Things always had to be smoothed over and peace kept at all costs. She said that fights between them were unthinkable, too awful to contemplate. There seemed to be a fear of some terrible explosion lurking in her unconscious. After a few sessions I could point out to her that she seemed to be saying that everything had to be peaceful and perfect or else everything would explode. She reluctantly agreed. The explosiveness seemed somehow to connect to her own angry side, while keeping the peace, or suffering in silence related to the part of her that coped on the surface in the home. She complained to me a lot about others and took a victim or martyr position. So it turned out that an important pair of opposites for Mary was victim and persecutor, or angry attacking person. She felt angry inside for having been put down so much in her life. She had been at the bottom of the family hierarchy and then she was also bottom of the classroom hierarchy. This angry side wanted to attack the parents, siblings and teachers in the world who had humiliated her. But that was too frightening because of her own upbringing, so she imagined that others were going to attack her instead. She even responded to me as though I was going to attack her.

Like many other women, Mary had real objective experiences of being a victim. At home she was expected to hold everything together, get the bills paid, feed everyone, keep the place tidy. Even in her work she was always looking after other people. Her own needs were not getting met. At the same time she was treated like a child. By being timid, she did at least get some nurturing, albeit of a patronizing kind. But she was also unconsciously playing the victim. This was an easier role than that of the angry woman, who might be attacked in return, rejected or simply misunderstood. 'Women as victims' is such a common and acceptable image in our society that it can feel more comfortable than being in touch with and expressing real needs. It also stopped Mary having to take full responsibility for her actions. Things seemed just to happen to her. It was 'nothing to do with her' that she ended up in a particular relationship or got pregnant.

It was hard for Mary to own the parts of herself that she didn't accept. But identifying an angry side was a vital step on her journey towards growth and change. Her voice would actually deepen when she expressed that side.

Louise

Louise seemed to want to do all the work of the second stage of identifying themes for herself. She was so scared of being vulnerable and of having anyone else 'feed' her, even with ideas, that she would talk non-stop and make it difficult for me to say anything at all. This made it hard to point out connections between things she said and to suggest some themes. She was also very definite about her opinions as to what was wrong with her marriage and saw counselling mainly in terms of improving her relationship with her husband. At first she had wanted to use counselling to help her diet, but she did acknowledge that her compulsive eating was a symptom of other underlying dissatisfactions.

The first few sessions seemed to focus mainly on discharging all her dissatisfactions with the marriage, with herself and with life. This was clearly a great relief to her and some trust was built up in those sessions. But it took quite a long time before we could find some themes for Louise actually to 'take in'. She did agree that she was always giving out to others, nurturing them and getting very little back for herself. But at first she would say that the situation was fine because she had so much. She had a lovely house, a car, beautiful children. She was lucky, so why should she be so miserable? Then she expressed feelings about her husband not respecting her and wondered whether he was seeing another woman. It was important not to collude with her by agreeing how awful her husband seemed to be, but I did show that I took very seriously what Louise often described as 'little' problems.

As she talked about her hurt and her longing for his affection and approval, we began to talk about the 'little' Louise who had never been properly understood. Then there was the 'big' Louise who was powerful, in control, and taking care of everyone else. She was able to laugh at the connections between 'bigness' in body and 'bigness' in terms of power and control. Actually her bigness, that she thought she hated, had a desirable side too. And maybe being small or thin could be scary. Being thin might not be the solution to all her problems after all. In fact under all those protective layers of fat there was a little Louise who was very needy and demanding of attention, approval and love.

We then started to talk in terms of needing to take care of the little Louise. This was a useful concept for her as she referred to it herself a number of times afterwards, and indeed throughout the counselling. She had never thought of herself as having a needy child actually inside her. It also became clear that it was this unsatisfied child that was doing the bingeing. Most of the time Louise was in control, of her diets, of her body, of the home, of her family. But being in control meant that she didn't get nurtured, so for her the issues of nurturing and being nurtured were connected with the other opposites of control and lack of control. There was also the issue of power. When in control Louise was powerful, when out of control, completely powerless. Yet ironically, it was that powerless, child side that ate all the food to make her physically big in order to protect the little Louise inside.

At this point in the counselling, after about two months, Louise decided that one of her aims in counselling was to find ways other than eating of getting nurturing for the 'little' side of her self. The opposite sides had been in conflict for so long, with one or other of them 'winning' or 'losing', that it was hard for Louise to see them both as valuable parts of herself, only seriously destructive if denied. Now they could help each other. They could learn to 'dance together'.

5 Exploring the Past: Understanding the Opposites and Inner Hierarchies

We shall not cease from exploration
And the end of all our exploring
Will be to arrive where we started
And to know it for the first time.

(T.S. Eliot, 'Little Gidding',
The Four Quartets)

This third stage both grows out of and is part of the stage of defining themes. In the last chapter we 'separated' out themes that are important for clients. In this one we look at where those themes came from. During this stage of counselling we explore one person's life (the client's) as though we were two detectives. Together the counsellor and the client search for clues, looking for the causes of her present-day splits and problems in the distant or recent past, for example, in early relationships with parents, in recent situations with friends or lovers, or even in the structures of society.

However, in counselling we are not trying to prove that a certain cause *alone* led to a certain effect. We are not conducting a scientific experiment. Rather we are trying to look differently at clients' lives, in ways that will help them to live their lives more fully. If understanding helps us to feel better about ourselves, then it works. It doesn't have to be a final, absolute, empirical truth.

Dropping Guilt

One way in which understanding helps people, especially women, is in stopping us blaming ourselves for everything. Many women and some men who come into counselling feel that there is something deeply wrong with themselves. Any problems that they have are seen as 'all their fault'. Our individualistic culture, which teaches us that 'anyone can get to the top if they personally strive hard enough' encourages self-blame if things go wrong. For women, there is also the additional burden of having been blamed for society's evils for thousands of years. This cultural 'blame' goes very deep and has been internalized even by modern women. In Judeo-Christian religions the female is associated with sex and sin much more than men are. It was Eve who tempted Adam in the garden of Eden, and today it is usually mothers who get blamed for their offspring's delinquency or drug-addiction. So often we hear women in 'failed' marriages saying 'It was all my fault. I just wasn't good enough for him. I wasn't attractive enough. I didn't try hard enough. There must be something wrong with me.' At first it rarely occurs to these women to put the blame outside themselves, to think that the husband could also be wrong or that their problems might come from other areas, such as unrealistically high expectations of marriage. All too often the woman's automatic response is to blame herself.

Counselling is not about blame. It is about recognizing anger towards other people and situations that have been repressed. So it may seem that 'blaming one's parents' is a vital stage for clients to go through. Eventually however, they will be able to see the strengths as well as the weaknesses of those parents, their love as well as their rage. As mentioned before, we do not see the parents as the final cause of any client's problems; we recognize that those parents themselves have been deeply affected by the patriarchal, hierarchical world most of us live in. Putting anger outside ourselves on to others, such as husbands, parents, teachers, stops us turning it all on ourselves. Anger turned in on the self often leads to depression. Eventually our search for understanding leads us back to the patriarchal and hierarchical ways of thinking and organizing society. If we want to blame something, we should blame the patriarchal structures underlying our societies, not individual people. These are what we need to change, and these are what we describe as the enemy.

Following the Clues

Our journey of discovery is led by the client. She is the one holding the thread as we venture into the labyrinth of her unconscious, of her past, of her fears and hopes. As a counsellor I just provide the structure of the labyrinth itself, the possible pathways (see Figure 5). Some may be dead ends. Others may at first seem to just go round and round. The often tangled ball of thread the client clutches when first coming to counselling is the muddle of her present conflicts and confusions. Gradually it is unravelled as we explore deeper, following clues, events remembered from childhood, phrases endlessly repeated by a scolding mother, images of half-forgotten rooms, etc. Anything may be a clue to finding causes for psychological problems. It could be a childhood memory or a more recent event. It could be something in the present. The way a persons sits, or the clothes that they wear, can all provide clues. Phrases that they keep repeating

Figure 5   *The labyrinth*

such as 'I wouldn't know about that', or 'It doesn't bother me', can be vital clues about a client's low idea of their own worth, or their rebelliousness. The way that the counsellor helps a client to notice the clues and follow them depends very much on skills and personal style. A feminist counsellor, like others, would be looking out for repeating patterns, but would often find that the client notices them first. The counsellor provides an environment that facilitates the noticing of clues; she does not impose her interpretations on an unprepared client. They are *both* the detectives.

Some clients, however, imagine that there must be one particular event that will explain everything. 'Being dropped or abandoned by mother' is one of the events people expect to have been traumatic. Being sexually assaulted or attacked is another obvious trauma. And for many people such events, unfortunately, really did take place. There often really *is* a monster lurking in the depths of the labyrinth. Naturally people are very scared of even remembering such awful situations, so the journey may indeed be filled with dread. As the client remembers more and more about childhood, and comes closer to the feared memory, she may well stop coming for counselling. The pain is just too much to bear. Using the feminist rhythm model, I often find that it helps to alternate sessions full of heaviness and painful memory with lighter sessions filled with positive aspects of the present and with humour.

Splits in the Family

For most clients there isn't usually a single event that caused all present problems. It is more likely that the continual humiliations of childhood did their damage in a more subtle way. It may be a whole string of abandonments by a busy mother, not just one parting, and the way the child learnt to cope with these may be the way she copes with any partings or losses today. In addition to traumatic events there may have also been the more general on-going splits in family behaviour and thought. For example, in one family it seemed that one sister had been labelled 'stupid' and the other one 'clever'. They both lived up to these labels, with the 'stupid' one feeling inferior to the other, marrying young and never feeling good enough for her father or husband. The other felt that she always had to perform well at school and then university or she wouldn't be loved. She felt that she was only loved for her achievements, not for herself. The split came first from the either/or culture that we live in. People are divided even at school into 'clever' ones and 'stupid' ones. It is not recognized that these are false opposites expressed within a framework of hierarchical thinking. And the children internalize the opposites in the same extreme divided form. They actually feel either clever *or* stupid. In reality everyone is both 'clever' and 'stupid' in different aspects of their lives at different times.

In families there can also be splits between members in order to help children feel 'different' in our highly individualized culture. If both sisters are seen as clever then how will they be distinguished? If they are opposites, then at least they have their own areas of importance, and everyone needs to feel important and special. But modern society does not foster the ability to appreciate and accept all the opposite sides of the same person. It cannot accept the different ways in which everyone is 'clever' *and* 'stupid', succeeding and failing. Progressive educationalists have tried to value all sides of children at school, but this holistic approach to the person does not fit comfortably with our hierarchical, capitalist world.

When working with clients it soon becomes clear which of a pair of opposites a person has been 'put in' by family and friends. She usually tells the counsellor, 'I was the bright one', or 'the pretty one', or 'the one expected to take care of everyone', or 'the good one', or 'the naughty one'. Often lurking beneath the main opposite is the feared 'other side'. A woman who was always the 'good girl' often has a terror of her 'bad' side. A person who feels that she must always be the best, be perfect or be top, usually has a fear that if she isn't, she must be a total failure. These splits are very common in our culture, but they have usually been reinforced by parents, anxious for their children to do 'better' than them, or to make up for their own 'weaknesses' or failures.

Splits in Everyday Life
Everyone seems to have experienced some kind of hierarchy in their past, either in the family or outside, e.g. at school. These hierarchies tend to be internalized to some degree by everyone in the culture, regardless of specific childhood experiences. A girl treated equally at home is still likely to find herself looking for a husband to give her status, like her more traditionally brought up friends. She is still likely to suffer from harassment and being patronized by men. So although childhood experiences are a vital part of our quest for clues and causes, they are not the only area of interest. We also look within the language, within the culture, within the organization of everyday life. The pattern a person uses to deal with the hierarchies may have been ingrained from childhood. Some withdraw, others attack, but the feelings of inferiority and rage, even if repressed, are still usually present.

In our journeys of exploration with clients it may help to get a picture of the hierarchies and power relationships in the family, including the attitudes to boys and girls, males and females. Women clients often realize, when talking about childhood in counselling, that their brothers got more attention than they did, and this realization uncovers a repressed feeling of great unfairness and injustice.

Most children have a strong sense of justice and struggle desperately hard for equality in relationships, and yet few achieve it. Rage about unfairness is usually buried in adult life. The unfairness may not only relate to gender, but to favouritism, or to having been an older sibling always left in charge of younger children, or to being blamed for everything. There is often resentment simply at the enormous power that parents wield over their children. Sometimes this is direct and even oppressive as in 'Do as I say', or it could be confusing, such as 'Do what you want, but I won't like it.'

It can be helpful for clients to discover where some of their own resentful feelings came from. Some clients take to this detective work with great enthusiasm; one woman started 'interrogating' her entire family, aunts and all, about her childhood. In fact we eventually agreed to curb this keenness for fear of unnecessarily hurting family members. It doesn't always help the client actually to confront a mother or other relative with her past patterns of rejection or neglect. Feelings about rejection or neglect can be expressed in the counselling session. For Louise, just realizing that her present feelings of rage at never being taken seriously were connected to a mother who always laughed at her helped her feel better about herself. She was only then able to believe that she had a right to be taken seriously, once she knew that there was a good reason for her problem. People usually feel reassured when they have found reasons for things.

Other clients either cannot or don't want to remember much about their childhoods, so the clues have to come more from the present. For some, childhood may have been too painful to remember, and vital clues may take years to uncover. In short-term counselling there may not be time to return to important early traumas, but that does not mean that we cannot work with current patterns of behaviour or feelings that may have been originally 'caused' by forgotten situations.

Some Techniques for Exploring the Past

Talking about early memories of family relationships and family expectations and demands can be a vital part of counselling. Sometimes just talking brings up forgotten memories, but for some people it may help to use particular techniques. Asking people what is the first thing they remember can provide a vital clue to their patterns. The very first event remembered is likely to crystallize all the forces going on around them at the time. For one person it was being chased by a dog, for another being read to by father, for another, being left in hospital. These memories all fitted in with later patterns. For example, the woman who remembered being chased by a dog was always very anxious and frightened of other people, especially men, and especially men who were interested in her sexually. It turned out later that she had actually been sexually touched by her own father, but she could not remember that event at first. What is actually remembered is not always the first or most important trauma or positive incident in the person's life, but it may be symbolic of a whole emotional atmosphere. The dog represented dangerous, violent sexuality.

Clients can be encouraged to relax and freely associate, letting any thoughts come into their minds. Sometimes a guided fantasy back to childhood can help them remember forgotten events or feelings. The client would be asked to imagine herself, for example, coming in from the garden to hear her parents talking about her. What were they saying? What did she feel?

We can also use phrases from the present to move into the past. When a client keeps saying 'I must try harder', or 'It's no good complaining', the counsellor can ask her 'Who is telling you that?' or 'Where did you hear that comment before?', and very often it turns out that a parent or sibling or teacher had continually made the same comment in her childhood. Or she may have made her own decision to, for example, give up trying, or complaining, at an early age. Then it might be helpful to ask her when she started feeling that way or whether she remembered feeling or thinking differently.

Attitudes involving splits such as 'either I'm strong, tough and coping *or* I am completely weak and useless' are often perceived by clients as the truth. They say things like 'But that's the way it is, isn't it?' Only when the counsellor helps her explore where she heard it first, where it had come from, does she realize that it was learnt.

Change through Understanding Inner Hierarchies

Understanding why and how we learnt certain ways of thinking and being can stop us blaming ourselves, but it can also help us realize that they can be unlearnt. It makes change feel more possible. After all, we were just copying or reacting to what our parents, siblings, friends, teachers, said and thought and felt. And their attitudes were largely the product of a particular social system.

Recognizing the powerful influence of childhood on the adult does not have to leave us feeling pessimistic and believing that what we are today is totally determined by the time we are five. Feminists are not only concerned with the past, but also with the future. We are all processes, not things. We are in a constant state of change and development in rhythms and cycles. We are deeply affected by our personal and collective pasts, but there is also much that we can change. We need both a realistic pessimism and a healthy optimism. We do not think in either/or terms. Childhood *and* the present are both important for personal understanding and change. The present patriarchy can be changed. A different future can be imagined. But first we need to understand our present inner hierarchies.

Strategies for Understanding Inner Hierarchies

Non-directive Strategies

In my experience all clients have acceptable and less acceptable (to them) sides of themselves, a split which expresses their inner hierarchies. To understand these it can help simply to start noticing the unacceptable side. In non-directive counselling we are simply feeding back to the clients what they have said, perhaps in a slightly different way. We are following closely the client's own train of thought, not giving them our own interpretations or suggesting that they *do* an exercise. During this stage I listen to clients as they talk about their present or past lives. Then I *feed back* to them their own comments about behaviour or feelings that *they* describe as being not acceptable. For example, if a client says that she thinks that she 'shouldn't feel so angry' or 'should *always* be strong', I may say 'It sounds as if you are saying to me that it's not OK to feel angry', or 'Only your strong side is acceptable, but not your vulnerable side.' As far as possible I use their words.

I encourage clients to discover for themselves just how unacceptable this 'side' of them feels. I might use humour, exaggerating how absolutely awful it is to be angry, or sad! I might say 'Of course, we are supposed to be happy *all* the time! That is what you seem to be saying.' This often leads to a shock of recognition.

I might ask an open-ended question, like 'What makes you think that you should always be happy?' This kind of question often leads on to talking about friend's and/or parents' expectations, or even what 'society' expects. It might be useful then to ask them to focus on specific incidents such as a time when a friend didn't want to meet the client because she was not being her usual 'cheerful' self.

I also feed back to them comments concerned with wanting approval or fitting in with people that they view as 'above' or superior to them, such as parents, bosses or husbands or even dominating friends. I might say 'You seem to be saying that what your husband thinks is more important than what you think.'

Directive Strategies

In directive counselling the counsellor plays a more active part. For example, I might ask a client to 'put' her unacceptable side on a chair and talk to it. Afterwards she could sit on that chair herself and immerse herself in that side. If it was her sad side I might encourage her to curl up and remember a time when she felt sad in the past. In this situation I am like the director of a play in which all the parts are played by the client. I am in a sense 'ordering her around', but the aim is to help her understand the different sides of herself better. And this kind of work would follow from what the client had said earlier in the session, e.g. 'I should always be happy'.

I might ask her if she remembers hearing parents or others saying to her what she is now telling me, e.g. 'I'm so much luckier than others so I *should* never feel miserable.' I might ask her to write down things that she had been told as a child that she 'should' do or feel. It may be that one command was more important than others. Sometimes I then pretend to be the parent giving her that one command, telling her that she 'should be happy', for example. The client can 'play' herself as a child and we can see how she reacts. Often parental 'shoulds' bring out the rebellious response of 'If you tell me I must, then I won't.' I might ask the client to play both sides of her, the parent and the child side. They can argue with each other and thereby get to understand each other better. For people with strong parental 'shoulds' in their heads, the child side is often unacceptable. The inner hierarchy of the parent/child has been deeply ingrained, and much work may need to be done in helping the client to accept the child side as being just as valuable as the parent side. Sometimes I say to clients quite directly: 'It's OK to feel sad', or 'It's OK to feel angry with your mother', adding 'It's quite understandable' or 'most people feel like that sometimes.'

This leads to another directive role, which is that of the teacher. I may tell clients: 'We all have a child side still within us. Things that happened to us as children can still go on affecting us, especially if we have deliberately forgotten them, because they hurt too much. The child side is where our desires and wants come from. The child is saying "I want" while the inner parent or conscience is saying "I should." We need both.' Such teaching may be appropriate after a client has talked about some 'unacceptable' desires or feelings, or has expressed a belief that when you grow up you are not supposed to have childish thoughts or feelings. Sometimes instead of parent and child, we talk of the 'big you' and the 'little you', and in the course of counselling I may often refer to these two sides. 'Now it sounds as though it's the "little you" talking'; 'The big one does not need to dominate or kill off the little one. Without energy from the little one the big one would simply be a robot.'

Specific questioning is another directive way of exploring the inner hierarchies. For example, 'What was your earliest memory?', or 'Who told you that you weren't good enough?' 'Do you remember when you first experienced that feeling of disappointment?' 'Does this situation of rejection remind you of any other similar incidents in the past?'

Guided fantasies and free association as described above (p. 63) can also be useful directive strategies. When a client is very relaxed I might encourage her just to say whatever comes into her head: memories, images, words, feelings. This can often lead clients into remembering long-forgotten and perhaps quite significant childhood experiences, which can then be understood.

Julia

When Julia starting talking about her childhood she made it sound very rosy. They had plenty of money and took family holidays twice a year. Julia remembered these well and seemed to have had her happiest memories away from home. Was there a clue here? Was home more of a strain? She insisted at first that her childhood had been happy all the time. She said that her parents were very liberal and had few rules. Julia felt that her problems started after leaving home, but because she was so anxious to please me she reluctantly began to examine her childhood more closely.

She remembered Daddy always being in the study, and herself having to be quiet. She remembered Mother reading poetry to her. And then there was the time when Mother burned the dinner. Was this a clue about Mother's own sense of inadequacy? In fact Julia remembered many times when Mother's cooking went wrong. Apparently she used to get really flustered and upset, as though it were the end of the world. Julia told me that her mother was pretty useless in the kitchen. In fact she was a 'pretty hopeless mother'. Julia seemed to despise her mother, but talked about her with little feeling at first.

Then during her third session Julia suddenly began to cry. She said, 'Perhaps my childhood wasn't all that wonderful after all. But I feel I don't have a right to be sad about it. After all we had everything we wanted and very loving, easy-going parents.' I said, 'It seems as though you feel you're not allowed to have any bad feelings about your childhood, because you were well off in some ways. Didn't you have a right to be sad sometimes?' She told me that she was always expected to be cheerful and to think how lucky she was. But actually she had been miserable sometimes. Her parents had often missed her school shows and that had hurt a lot. Once she had run away and they hadn't even noticed. As Julia followed the clues of her memories, we began to develop a different, more mixed, less rosy picture of her childhood. We found that Julia had been categorized in her family as the cheerful and competent one: she had been expected to cope. Less fuss was made of her, while apparently it was her two younger brothers who 'had problems' and needed attention. It had always been assumed that she would be all right.

The clues led to example after example of times when Julia had actually felt neglected, but the message from parents had always been: 'How lucky you are compared to all those poor people! You should be grateful for having so much', so Julia had repressed her own hurt and anger. I had to encourage her to feel that she did indeed have a right to those sad and angry feelings, despite her advantages. Julia was also politically active on behalf of disadvantaged people in her area, and felt it was an indulgence and even ideologically 'incorrect' to spend time on her own problems: surely other people's problems were always so much worse than hers. So the message she had taught herself as a result of childhood experiences was 'other people matter more than I do.'

This realization turned out to be an important landmark in our journey. After it, Julia started looking for more clues in her present relationships and situations where the same pattern emerged. She was always listening to friends' problems and rarely talked about herself. She was always treating men as though they were more important than her, despite her feminist beliefs.

Julia had already told me that her brothers had had more attention than she had, but one day she remembered how Tom, two years younger than herself, had been given a toy car for Christmas. Julia had hidden it because of her jealousy. She began to talk about her feelings of envy and rage towards Tom in particular, and how she thought her mother preferred him to her. We then began to uncover more clues about her jealous feelings, and the way Julia tried so hard to please the mother who still preferred Tom. Whatever she did never seemed good enough for her mother. As the mother herself 'hadn't felt good enough', she projected those inferior feelings on to Julia to live out her own fears of failure. So Julia was constantly being given double messages. On the one hand she was being told 'You are competent and good but you are never going to be good enough for me, so you are also a failure.' The day Julia realized that whatever she did would never be good enough for her mother was another vital landmark for her. She kept saying to me after that: 'I don't need her approval; I don't need her approval.' It was ironic that at first it had seemed that only her father's approval mattered, when in the end her mother had turned out to be just as important. She also realized that the part of her that wanted to please mother was undermining her. To 'please' mother meant to fail. Julia had been caught in an impossible contradiction and had completely lost touch with who *she* actually was, or what *she* actually wanted, or even what *she* actually felt. Julia had even thought that she was happy when actually she was sad.

Mary

At first Mary could remember very little about her childhood. It had been very strict, but she could not remember her parents quarrelling. In that family all the anger had been repressed. Mary thought that she had been well behaved, as there wouldn't have been any point in being naughty. No point? Was there a clue here? Had Mary given up making demands, sticking up for herself even before she started? Mary would shrug her shoulders and say 'It's no use' several times in each session. We looked at where that expression had come from, but Mary insisted that it was her own and had come from her own experience. Even if you asked for what you want, she thought, you wouldn't get it, so why ask? Other people usually win, so why fight?

What were the sort of things she might ask for, I wondered? This proved to be a useful path to take her down. At first it was hard for Mary to get in touch with what she felt and wanted, but eventually after spending time at home writing lists of 'what I want' she had some clues. She found that she wanted space and time for herself. She wanted to be listened to, taken seriously and treated as an adult. Just stating these wants was an important first step. Then Mary was able to use some of the wants as clues to explore where her feelings of depression and powerlessness came from. She began to remember many times, both in childhood and recently, when she had been interrupted while talking. She had always been the quiet little one in the background. She had been the bottom of the family hierarchy as the youngest, always being told by others what to do. 'They' were all bigger than her, so what was the point in questioning or disagreeing with them. No wonder that she had made an early decision to give up trying.

It was easier with Mary to look for more recent clues to her problems. She described incidents when her husband had decided what they were going to do, when and how, without consulting her. Once again she was not being listened to, and she felt dominated. On exploration it turned out that she was really angry about being bossed around so often. Her needs were not being met. Her husband didn't do the things she wanted him to do, such as putting up those kitchen shelves. It felt as if the hierarchy between them was rigid and oppressive, perhaps like the hierarchy in her own family. Mary wasn't sure about this connection and just went on insisting that her parents were happy and never quarrelled. She could not easily express her own anger, as she had no model from her own parents of people expressing feelings honestly to each other.

As Mary told me more and more of the things she wanted from her marriage, from friends, from life itself, she began to express more and more resentment at not having met those wants in the past. When we looked closely at some of the particular situations in which Mary had not got what she wanted, it turned out that she had so expected to fail that she hadn't even asked properly in the first place. Mary had deeply internalized the hierarchies of her family, but she had also internalized the school hierarchies. She had been slow to read and write, and soon found herself very behind at school. Once again she stopped trying and simply found a quiet seat at the back of the classroom. She believed that she was dumb or stupid, and even her family put that label on her by not expecting her to write letters or read anything to them. They just assumed that 'Mary wouldn't be able to cope with that.' She described many incidents when she was able to avoid reading or writing, or putting herself forward in public life. She had developed a massive inferiority complex.

One of the clues as to where this complex came from was her repetition of the phrase 'I can't . . .', in session after session. When I suggested that she said 'I won't' instead, Mary was shocked at first. This seemed an especially important clue for the next stage of her journey. Yes, it gradually became clear that she was actually *refusing* unconsciously to do things. At least that felt more powerful for her. She was not a passive victim, but a rebel. During one session we talked angrily about the limits and injustices of the education system and the effect of early labelling on children. After that Mary went off to sign up for some literacy classes.

In another session we talked about the injustices in the way mothers and wives are treated by society. She became very angry about being expected to hold down a full-time job and still keep a home running. Her husband thought that he did a lot to help, but she was the one who felt ultimately responsible. Her ways of rebelling turned out to be quite ingenious. She would go quiet for days or refuse to have sex, or tidy away his books in places where he wouldn't easily find them. She resented the hierarchy and felt like a slave, but didn't dare face him directly with her demands or requests for changes. As a start, however, seeing herself as the angry rebel gave a boost to her morale and helped her recognize that she had more power than she had previously realized.

Louise

Louise remembered a lot about her childhood, and also had a number of vivid dreams during the time we worked together. Dreams are a vital source of clues, but need to be interpreted in relation to the particular journey and stage reached by the individual. The first clues that we followed were connected with weight, appearance and attractiveness, as these were the issues she had brought to counselling. Louise was afraid that if she didn't lose weight her husband would leave. He was always criticizing her. She gave me many examples of times when she had dressed up specially and he had criticized some aspects of her appearance, hair, shoes, make-up or clothes. I asked if these situations reminded her of others, in her childhood perhaps. It turned out that her mother had also constantly criticized her.

Louise remembered a particular instance when she had gone shopping with her mother, who had laughed at Louise's struggles to get into a tight skirt. Louise was 13 at the time, and had felt dreadfully humiliated. It seemed that her obsession with weight had started around that time. As we explored further it became clear that puberty had been very traumatic, and then Louise realized that it was when she was thirteen that her father had left to live with another woman. She didn't remember having any feelings about it at the time. Was there a clue here? She had apparently been close to her father even to the extent that her mother had been jealous — but she didn't feel anything when he left? Was there guilt? Rage? It felt like a blank wall. There were no more memories, no feelings.

And then Louise had a dream, in which her father had driven up to the entrance of their old house, where Louise was playing with her sister. She ran over to the car and kissed him. It had felt good. They talked for a while about her counselling. Then he kissed her and drove off. When she woke up Louise had felt a tremendous sensation of relief. She had cried and cried, and then experienced some anger towards her mother for 'blaming' her for everything, including father's departure. Previously it had seemed that father was all bad and mother was all good. Mother had been on a pedestal for Louise. Now it was possible to explore all the negative feelings for mother that had previously been repressed and turned against herself. Unconsciously she had hidden them in order to protect her mother, and somehow her grief at her father's leaving had seemed disloyal to mother and had not been allowed into consciousness. The dream had been a vital event and landmark in Louise's journey.

The next set of clues led us towards her mother. Louise remembered being blamed by her for things her younger sister had done. And what had hurt most was that her mother hadn't believed that she was telling the truth. One day she burst into tears and said 'It's all so unfair. I hate my mother.' Then she stopped suddenly and a pained look came over her face; 'I've never said that before', she admitted. I suggested that she wrote a letter to her mother without actually posting it. In it she could express all the negative hateful feelings without hurting her mother, for most of those feelings were connected to her mother as she had been when Louise was a child. I also pointed out that there was still a positive side to mother that could be addressed as well, perhaps in a later one. But at that point Louise was not ready to experience positive feelings. She was too involved in the negative. She went away from the session and wrote pages and pages of resentment, disappointment, blame, rage and simple dislike.

In a psychological sense, Louise had never completely separated from her mother. Understanding where her self-criticism, guilt and repressed anger came from helped her to put 'blame' outside rather than towards herself. But it also helped her separate from her mother. Previously she had felt too guilty about her closeness to her father and her 'secret powerfulness' to detach herself. By over-identifying with mother, unconsciously she could stop those frightening feelings coming into consciousness. For they were her own feelings, feelings that could be 'against' mother as well as 'for' her. There had been a very rigid hierarchy between Louise and her mother, against which she had only unconsciously rebelled. But now mother could come right down off the pedestal and at first be seen as 'down there'. Much later in the counselling, the positive sides of mother were also returned to consciousness and Louise could see her as the equal mixture of negative and positive aspects that she 'really' was. It was also possible to explore some of the social clues about her mother's own feelings of inferiority and need to 'keep up with the Jones', etc., and to recognize that her mother had been affected by the marriage hierarchy in which the husband was boss. When she had got older and therefore in his eyes less attractive, he preferred a younger woman. She too was oppressed by patriarchy, but her rage against it had been impotent, largely repressed, distorted into obsessive house-cleaning and into blaming her daughters, especially Louise.

All her life the message Louise had been telling herself was, 'I must protect mother (and everyone else) from my anger and power.' It just didn't seem possible that they could both be powerful. It had always felt as though it must be 'either/or', 'Either mother is powerful or I am. If I am powerful, then mother will be destroyed.' So although Louise came across on the surface as a powerful, competent woman, inside she had convinced herself that she was really weak in order to protect her mother. And in particular she had to repress her sexuality, for that had been too threatening for her insecure mother years ago, when Louise was becoming a woman. Yet to be fully powerful also means to allow the full feelings of vulnerability which Louise had not allowed herself before the crucial dream. Her earlier 'weak' side had just been repressed anger, not genuine vulnerability.

As Louise went on working through counselling she was able to follow the spiral path of 'powerfulness, yet allowing vulnerability' and get to know the two sides better. For Mary her apparent 'weakness' also turned out to be a source of strength, and for Julia her sadness as well as her cheerfulness began to feel more 'reasonable'. All of them benefited from exploring childhood memories.

6 Dissolving the Inner Hierarchies and Facing Ambivalence: Accepting the Opposites

> That which shrinks, must first expand.
> That which fails, must first be strong.
> That which is cast down, must first be raised.
> Before receiving there must be giving
> This is called the perception of the nature of things.
> Soft and weak overcome hard and strong.
>
> (Lao Tsu, *Tao te Ching*)

Ambivalence

Having recognized some of the main themes and 'inner hierarchies' in which parts of ourselves have been rejected, the next task is to accept fully those parts. In the last chapter we looked at the 'causes' of these splits betweeen opposite parts of ourselves, whereby one side usually becomes unacceptable. Understanding why we feel the way we do seems to help, but it is rarely enough. We need really to accept those rejected opposites as parts of ourselves. We need to acknowledge and respect the sad side as well as the happy side, the angry side as well as the gentle side, the vulnerable side as well as the strong side.

For entire lifetimes people have experienced these opposites within them in a hierarchical way, with one side being on top and the other seen as inferior. We have felt that one was good and the other bad. We have felt that the 'strong' side must control the 'weak'. In counselling we aim to dissolve the hierarchical relationship of superior and inferior while keeping a clear awareness and appreciation of the differences between the opposite sides.

Instead of assuming that there must be a hierarchical relationship between different sides of ourselves, I use the ancient model of constant rhythmic change between opposites. So a client who is depressed because the sad side of life has not been accepted can learn to accept the rhythm of life between happiness (outgoing energy) and sadness (in-going energy). This is just like the movement from spring, through summer and autumn, to the death-like stage of winter, and then there is the rebirth of a new spring. Indeed many people in countries with definite seasons do get depressed in the winter and come out of it in the spring. We all have our own yearly, monthly and even daily rhythms, and this will be explored in the next chapter. We need to flow with these rhythms rather than fight them. We can be in quite opposite states of being at different times, but cannot usually be in opposites at the same time. This is why ambivalence is so hard to understand, let alone accept. But the rhythm model does allow for ambivalence by adding the dimension of *time*: we can be strong one day and vulnerable the next.

This model makes it easier for us to accept emotionally the previously less valued sides of ourselves. Sadness is more acceptable if it is not seen as locked in eternal combat with happiness. If sadness 'wins', we think that it must last for ever, so we are desperate to get rid of it. Each state is seen as *either* misery for ever *or* ecstatic joy for ever, like heaven and hell. Of course we can expect to vary between the two!

In our relationships too we are brought up to believe that *either* we love someone *or* we hate them, *either* they are perfect and superior to us *or* they are useless and inferior to us. In the same way that the rhythm model can help us to accept opposite sides within ourselves, so it can help us in our relationships to accept that one day our parents, friends, colleagues can be 'good' and another day 'bad'. One day they might be in control, strong, 'parental' and another day they could be the one being 'looked after'.

Counselling is one area where these patterns can be examined and questioned. In particular the relationship between the counsellor and client is very important in the process of change from hierarchy to rhythm, from seeing a person as all 'good' or all 'bad' to an acceptance of ambivalence, to having resentments and appreciations for the same person.

The Middle Phase of Counselling

Ambivalence towards the Counsellor

It is during the middle period of counselling that issues to do with ambivalence usually emerge. Ambivalence and paradox, or the holding of two opposites in one is like the Holy Grail in the centre of the labyrinth. It is the still centre in the middle of the spiral. Having journeyed inwards on her path of self-discovery it is the point at which a client realizes that she is OK just as she is, with all the different sides, including the previously unacceptable ones. She does in fact come to the place where she has actually been all her life but 'knows it for the first time'.

But to achieve this acceptance of her own 'paradoxical' nature she may first need to experience and recognize feelings of ambivalence towards other people or things, including the counsellor.

At first many clients think that the counsellor is wonderful. It may be the first time that they have been really listened to. There is often a fantasy that the counsellor is *totally* together and has sorted out all her problems. She may be seen as the perfect model of what the client should be like. Perhaps she is seen as the most 'right-on' feminist, or for other clients she may seem to have the perfect nuclear family. All kinds of longings and desires are projected by the client on to the counsellor. Some of these may be based in reality, as when a counsellor has pictures of her nuclear family displayed in the room where she sees clients. She may actually *be* more 'successful' in work or money terms. She may even have gone further in coming to terms with herself and accepting all the opposite sides. But usually these 'projections' contain something of the client's own desires and fantasies as well. The client often puts 'good' qualities, that she doesn't feel that she has, on to the counsellor. While she, the client, feels unsuccessful, the counsellor is seen as successful. While the client is unattractive, the counsellor is seen as attractive. While the client feels isolated and friendless, the counsellor is seen as having lots of friends and never being lonely. The splits are often in terms of all or nothing: the counsellor is seen as having it all and the client is seen as having nothing. The counsellor is seen as all-powerful and the client feels herself to be totally powerless.

For some clients it works the other way round. The counsellor is identified more with the enemy, or the 'bad' side. She may be experienced as cruel and rejecting, or as representing the establishment or status quo, as the 'bad' authority. Or she may even be seen as being useless and not helpful. Where she is experienced very negatively from the start, there may be a difficulty in starting the process of counselling at all. Clients may leave after just a few sessions. However, because of the hierarchical attitudes in our society, most clients believe that the counsellor knows best even if they don't like them very much. Counsellors tend to be put on some kind of pedestal by clients in the early stages of counselling, even when they are disliked.

But in the middle stage, clients often start to see 'negative' or less powerful aspects of the counsellor. It may be that the counsellor makes an interpretation that just doesn't fit. She might be late one day or make some clichéd remark that missed the point of what the client was feeling. She might look tired or ill. Often during this middle phase I have had clients suddenly start to be concerned about me or to 'notice' that I look tired. Even if I am not actually tired, it is important that they are able to show their awareness of the 'other' side of me. They might notice dust on a shelf, or crumples in a shirt. There can often be considerable hostility towards the counsellor during this stage.

Many clients feel ambivalent about their own feelings of wanting the perfect mother, counsellor. They both want it, and don't. They want her to be powerful, but resent it. They want her to be 'up there' but they also want to pull her down. They want to believe she is perfect and superior but they also crave equality. Clients may stay away, unable at first to deal with this ambivalence. They may cover up their hostility by being extra 'nice'. They may start saying 'Thank you' after every session, or they might even bring presents. Sometimes it is possible to point out to clients what they are doing. It may even be necessary to say 'It's OK to feel angry with me sometimes.' This gives them *permission*, which most clients initially seem to need.

Humour can be very useful here too. With many clients I have laughed about the idea that I might be totally together, all-knowing or even perfect. It does indeed sound somewhat ridiculous when spelled out directly. But although a client might know with her 'head' that I am not perfect, she may go on emotionally wishing that I was for a long time.

It is particularly useful if the counsellor goes on holiday or is unavailable for a while during this period. This can give the client something specific to direct her feelings of anger and disappointment at. For discovering that one's counsellor, like one's mother, is not totally reliable, perfect or always available, is a deeply disappointing experience. We have to give up the childish idea of the perfect parent. We have to accept ambivalence. This can seem like a terrible 'let down'. Does it mean that the parent or counsellor is 'useless'? We may be tempted to think that 'If she isn't perfect, then she must be useless', or 'If she isn't *always* available, then she must *never* be available.' The counsellor needs to show the client, not only through words but through action too, that she is not at either extreme. She is usually 'good' but she can sometimes be 'bad'. Ambivalence can be seen as positive, even as 'natural', rather than as a 'second best' to perfection. The counsellor's own attitude is important here too. She needs to have fully accepted for herself the ambivalence of life.

The client may need to mourn the loss of the old hierarchical ways of thinking which have been so familiar and so comfortable as well as so deeply damaging. She needs to let go of the old way of being as one would let go of a parent who has died. Indeed it is often as if the old fantasy parent has indeed died. What remains are real flesh and blood humans who can be both 'good' and 'bad'. A useful technique at this stage is to ask clients to write down on a sheet of paper all their resentments and their appreciations of important figures in their lives. The mourning process usually begins with a denial of what is happening. Sometimes in counselling there is a feeling of stuckness or confusion at this point. Questions about direction such as 'Where are we going now?' often come up. They might even say 'I don't feel we are getting anywhere these days.'

Then there is often a dream or an event in waking life that is of a surprising nature. It might be a dream of the counsellor in some uncharacteristic situation. For example one client, who had previously felt very supported by me, dreamed that she turned up one day at my 'cottage in the country' (I actually live in the city) with her family, but I would only let them stay for a short time. I did not let them stay all night as she had expected me to do. Clearly she was recognizing the 'other' side of me, the side that has her own personal life, maybe very different from the one the client knew about or expected. Also she saw that I had a rejecting side as well as an accepting one. But the outcome of the dream was the realization that she could have some of my time but not all of it. I was no longer the perfect, ever-available 'parent'.

Another client had a dream at this stage of her counselling that she was with a group of acquaintances who were criticizing me and she was 'sticking up' for me to them. She had recognized negative feelings towards me, but had put them outside herself, as if they came from other people, and another side of her was arguing for my positive attributes. She coped with her ambivalence by creating a dialogue in her dream between the two attitudes. If the counsellor can be seen as both 'good' and 'bad', then, surely, so can the client. This dream did indeed mark a change in the client towards greater self-acceptance.

So many women (and some men) come to counselling with very low self-esteem that they often start seeing themselves as all 'bad' or 'worthless' and the counsellor, or their mother, as all 'good' or more valuable. By feeling ambivalence towards the counsellor, clients are freed to feel the 'good' as well as 'bad' sides of themselves. As they go through the process of mourning the perfect parent they cannot have, they can let out feelings that had previously been unacceptable. Anger is of particular importance at this stage. The client is furious that the counsellor, or indeed her own parent, lover, friend, is not what she wanted her to be. She resents her bitterly, She may even want to attack her, verbally or physically. It is vital that outlets for such strong feelings are found, and not all clients find it easy actually to shout at their counsellors or punch cushions in their presence. But the counsellor could make suggestions about ways of expressing this primal rage. Some people find it helpful to scream their lungs out while driving with the car windows closed. Others find isolated beaches or hill-tops to scream from. It can be vital to involve the body in this expression of emotion. For many clients a good game of squash or literally punching a cushion at home can be a great relief.

The surprisingly 'good' and 'powerful' feelings associated with this expression of fury often lead to vast untapped sources of energy. The feared 'bad' side doesn't feel so bad after all. The anger does however need to be contained, or the client will only have her worst fears confirmed, that her 'bad' side really is destructive. Rules about 'no physical violence' are essential in any counselling situation. It is also important that the counsellor does not reject her in any way at this very vulnerable time. Her fear of rejection is likely to come to the fore now. The counsellor needs to accept the anger, however directly or indirectly it is expressed, and let her know that it is OK, and that having these very understandable feelings does not make her an all-bad person.

The sense that a feminist counsellor has of being 'on the client's side' is particularly useful. People often feel ashamed and even humiliated by their own deep needs for the 'perfect' parent and their disappointment at not having her. By the time these painful feelings about the disappointing parent (counsellor) emerge, the client should feel respected by the counsellor. They both may have a sense of equality as two basically human people, in spite of their different roles. This sense of shared humanity can help to lay the ground for the realization of ambivalent feelings towards counselling and other people or events. It may sometimes be appropriate to share with the client that sense of loss of the perfect parent that we all experience to some extent. Unlike other animals, humans spend a long time being completely dependent; as such, all of us feel both a longing to escape from the humiliation of such dependency *and* a longing to return to its comfort. This is one of the paradoxes of being human.

After the expression of rage, mourning usually involves a great welling up of sadness and a sense of grief at what is lost. Clients may need to cry a lot. Often tears begin to flow as soon as the release of anger is allowed, as if they have just been waiting there for the anger to be expressed, or the two feelings can be very mixed up, even alternate. While anger is particularly difficult for women who are not brought up to express it at all, tearfulness is quite expected of women. It can be used to cover up anger.

Knowing our Feelings

Clients often describe feelings of muddle or confusion when there are unacceptable feelings waiting to be expressed. They may say that they don't know what they feel. Actually naming the feelings as they emerge can be an important part of accepting them. The labels 'sad' or 'angry' can be useful. Knowing what we feel is a vital part of accepting ourselves. When we don't accept feelings we often don't even know what they are.

At this stage I often ask clients to notice what they are feeling as they go about their daily lives. I suggest they stop when a new feeling is experienced and think about what it is. What name can they give the feeling? One client talked about becoming more 'intelligent' about feelings. We need to use our minds and our cognitive frameworks to help us fully accept and express feelings. People usually find that it is not enough just to let them all come out. It can help a client to write a diary describing feelings and noticing events that trigger certain particular emotions. Counselling is also a process of getting to know unfamiliar feelings and sides of ourselves. It is like befriending a new neighbour: gradually the unfamiliar becomes familiar. The first impressions settle into a set of expectations, a kind of intuitive knowing. When the feeling, like the neighbour, comes knocking on the door, you open it willingly to a familiar figure.

In counselling sessions there are many ways to help a client notice her feelings. The counsellor can simply ask 'How are you feeling now?' After she has been talking for ages about her husband and children, the counsellor could say 'But what about you? How do *you* feel?'

Many men have the opposite problem. They are more likely to be so concerned with their own view of reality that they find it hard to empathize with others' feelings. At the same time, for men, feelings are often connected with weakness and so are denied altogether in themselves and in anyone else. One of the fears in our 'either/or' society is that if we get closer to our feelings they will overwhelm us completely. We will become totally identified with those feelings and lose all capacity for reason. One client used to hold his breath at the start of every session. When this was pointed out he admitted that he was always scared at first. Not knowing exactly what feelings are going to emerge in the sessions is very frightening for people who have been used to keeping emotions down and under strict control. At first many clients decide beforehand exactly what they are going to talk about and try hard to be in control of the sessions, but during this middle stage, when trust has increased, many clients allow themselves to come unprepared and let their feelings and thoughts emerge more spontaneously.

Strategies for Encouraging Clients to Contact Deep Feelings

1 *Allowing silences* gives space for feelings to be actually experienced rather than simply talked about. It may often be necessary for

the counsellor to bring the client back to the 'here and now', to be really present in the room with her. She might say 'You don't have to talk' or 'Let's just *be* for a while.' One woman told me how difficult it was just to be alone with me simply as she is, metaphorically 'naked'. Usually she felt that she had to entertain me. Another woman felt that she was only valuable if she was doing something. Talking counted as doing something, so that was all right, but silences were terrifying. The silence is a powerful space for the client to discover a genuine self. It can be seen as the gap at the centre of the spiral or labyrinth. In that 'nothingness' or hole is in fact the whole being of the person. The 'empty vessel' they feared is actually full, of themselves. The hole is indeed holy.

2   *Being the container.* Out of the 'hole' may come surprising anger or joy or even tears. But there is often a sense that this 'hole' is itself neutral, neither 'good' nor 'bad', not some hard core of self that is essentially angry or sad or indeed any other permanent quality. This experience contradicts patriarchy's idea of a permanent essential, solid self. The image of the vessel or hole out of which and through which pour all the different states of being is far more 'feminine' than the 'masculine' image of a controlling ego. We do not need to identify totally with any particular feeling. Rather we can 'watch' feelings flow past in the ever-changing rhythms of daily life, while remaining their container. The paradox is that we are all both the container and the contained, both the vessel and the flow of feelings.

The counsellor can act as 'container' for the client's feelings while she is still unfamiliar with them. All the counsellor does is to sit and listen. While feelings are still scary or threatening for the client, the counsellor's presence may be needed to reassure her that all the feelings, and all the sides of herself, are acceptable. By listening non-judgementally, the counsellor is containing the client's feelings. Later on, as she gains confidence, the client will be able to contain her own feelings and watch and name them for herself as she goes through life. If the counsellor fully accepts the feelings, then so can the client.

3   *Watching and labelling the feelings.* Paradoxically, the more we try to control our feelings the less able we are to do so, because we are also denying them. When I encourage clients to let feelings out, acknowledge and accept them, I can help them to choose more rationally when it is appropriate to express them and when it isn't. The counsellor can discuss with the client how to choose when to show anger and when to hold it in. I might suggest going through the events of the past week and getting the client to say when expresssing anger would or would not have been appropriate. Once the client

knows her own feelings really well and is familiar with the emotions, she can allow herself to flow in and out of the different emotional states when it is appropriate. And when feelings emerge spontaneously a part of her can watch and say to herself, 'Ah, that is my frightened child side', or 'Ah, that is my anger again.' Knowing that she has the feeling does not mean automatically that she has to express it immediately. For example, frustration about a late train can be recognized without leading to screaming at the driver, but the client can learn to watch herself and know what she is feeling.

4   *Owning sides projected on to others.* In this stage the counsellor needs to encourage the client to absorb for herself some of the 'good' features she believed that her parents, counsellor, friends, etc. had. When she lets go of the fantasy of the perfect parent, she can still keep for herself parts of that parent. I may actually tell her that she too has power; she too has the ability to control and be in charge; she too has a great deal of knowledge and experience; she too has many other qualities that she had previously thought only belonged to the parent, or counsellor, or other authority figure. It is amazing how many clients at this stage suddenly decide that they want to be counsellors!

The counsellor can feed back to the client anything she says that indicates an envy or admiration of others. For example a client may say that she admires my freedom to work at home, material possessions, family or even imagined characteristics such as 'continual peace of mind'. I may then point out that the things she admires might actually be things that the client herself wants. She may not want to wear the particular clothes that I am wearing, but she might want more money to buy clothes that she really likes. I would ask her to decide exactly *what* things she really wants for herself. She may not want to be a counsellor, but she might want to be self-employed. She might not want to live in the particular flat or house that the counsellor lives in, but she might want to improve her own physical surroundings.

Often underneath admiration for the counsellor, friend or authority-figure is envy. And beneath the envy is an unfulfilled desire. Acknowledging those desires is a vital stage of counselling Sometimes feminist clients feel bad about wanting nice clothes, or socialist clients feel politically suspect if they want a big house or car. I may even explain to a client that denying those feelings actually makes them more powerful in the unconscious and distorts the desire into envy and sometimes hatred of those who have them. These feelings can contaminate political activity rather than enhance the more useful longing for justice and truth that motivate most progressive politics.

This is also the stage of beginning to accept previously denied 'negative' sides of ourselves that may have always been seen as belonging to other people. I might use a teaching strategy to teach the client about 'projection', e.g. friends, rather than oneself, being seen as envious or aggressive. A partner may be seen as *always* rejecting while the client sees herself as *never* rejecting. For one woman who felt rejected it turned out that unconsciously *she* had been rejecting her partner for not 'being good enough' for her, for years. When I suggested to her that she had been 'projecting' her own rejecting side on to him, she denied it at first, but later agreed that it was true.

Another couple divided into a 'victim' wife and a 'persecutor' husband. The woman came for counselling and eventually recognized a hidden side of herself that was also 'persecutory', always subtly criticizing her husband. I often have to add that this recognition of 'negative' sides within does not deny the reality of objectively real persecution. In fact the more we are all aware of the 'little Nazi' in every one of us, the less powerful these sides will be collectively. Everyone seems to have a side that would like to have had total control over mother and others as a baby. Yet so many people, especially women, have deeply ingrained self-images of being *always* nice and caring.

One social worker came to see me because she was fed up with always taking care of others. It became apparent that she had her self-identity tied up in being the 'good' person, helped by a Catholic upbringing. Yet she was having dreams about being covered in faeces, and desperately trying to scrape it off. Many clients have dreams based on a similar split. Our whole patriarchal culture and religion encourages this split and very often other groups of people get scapegoated for the 'negative' or 'dirty' side that we can't accept. There is usually some other, inferior group to be blamed for this 'dark' side. Racism feeds on such 'projections'. People of darker skin, of a lower class, or from another country or neighbourhood get labelled with all the 'shit' that belongs to us.

Julia

Julia had initially responded to me as though I were her father. She wanted to please me with her clever intellectual analysis of her problems and the whole relationship began on a mental level. But the side that she had ignored was the emotional side, belonging in her eyes to the mother or 'feminine' side. When we talked about her far-from-perfect childhood and her sadness and anger at being neglected, Julia needed a lot of encouragement to express her feelings. It was several weeks before she allowed herself to cry. And then she stopped quickly, saying that she didn't really have a good reason to cry. She felt that it would look as though she were blaming her mother for not giving her a perfect childhood. She began to give me lots of reasons why her mother hadn't had time to attend her school shows and how hard she had tried to be a good mother. It seemed to her that it was disloyal to complain about not having had the mother she wanted. Her mother had apparently invested a lot of emotional energy in the idea that childhood was a state of happy innocence. Being a liberal parent, she had put very few restrictions on Julia and her brothers, and Julia too had believed that childhood must be happy. The opposites were not acknowledged. There was only a one-sided view of childhood.

Julia had learnt a one-sided view of herself, the achiever, the coper, the strong one. As she got more in touch with the 'needy little girl' side of her, Julia began to respond to me more as her mother, her disappointing, neglectful mother. She was still eager to please, but there was an edge of defiance creeping in. She stopped automatically agreeing with what I said. One day she made a comment about my being lucky to have this kind of job. It soon became clear that she had built up a fantasy of my lifestyle and envied it. I seemed to her to be free and to have a rich artistic and social life. These were all things that she wanted. At first she denied having envious feelings, but one day she admitted that she was envious of what she assumed was my lifestyle. We then explored those elements of this fantasy that connected with things that she wanted for herself. I suggested that she wrote down a list of everything she wanted, at home, before the next session. She didn't do this 'homework', which seemed like a healthy rebellion against an imperfect mother, but could also have stemmed from a fear of looking at deep and long-neglected wants.

So I did a guided fantasy with her. I asked her to relax, breathe deeply for a while and then to imagine herself in five years' time. I asked her where would she be living, with whom, and so on. I encouraged her to express her wildest fantasies and desires, not to keep thinking about what was 'reasonable' as she usually did. It took a while for Julia to let go and really relax, but she found the fantasy. She was very surprised by what her imagination had created. It was a lifestyle very different from the one that she had previously thought that she wanted. She had two children and a husband and was also an artist, living in the country. It bore no relation to the academic world and political activity in the city that she had assumed that she *should* want. Julia herself noticed that the fantasy had been 'rather feminine', and not as achievement-orientated as she had expected. She began to cry after this fantasy, apparently with relief for having admitted those deep emotional wants, so alien to her intellectual, striving self. Impulsively I put my arms around her at this point, and she broke into fresh sobbing that came from even deeper within.

During this session she had shown both sides of herself and accepted the reality and value of the 'feminine' longings that she had despised for so long. Afterwards she was able to do the 'homework', and wrote down long prose poems about her desires that seemed to go on forever. It was as if an inner battle had ended and a truce been declared between the warring sides of 'masculine' and 'feminine' that had been split so hierarchically, deep in Julia's psyche. Admitting her longing for children, for example, did not mean that she would have to abandon the other side completely or rush off and grab the first available man. She needed to get to know and feel comfortable with the 'feminine' side *as well as*, not instead of, the 'masculine'. Eventually both sides could be equally valued.

Mary

For Mary the discovery of her angry, rebellious side had been a great relief. For a while, she went through a stage of only hating her husband and could find no good in him at all. She would spend whole sessions complaining about him, but still found it hard to show her anger through physical expression such as shouting. Her voice was still rather quiet. Then one day I really pushed her into shouting at a cushion that represented her husband. I kept asking her to speak louder, until I could sense that she was getting angry with me too. And then suddenly out came a hurt broken cry from her stomach. She sounded very upset for a moment, and then her voice came out deep and rather 'masculine'; 'I hate you', she said. Her face was distorted with rage and pain and her body began to shake. I put my hand on her knee and showed her that I could cope with her feelings and that it was all right to be angry.

Then she burst into tears and said 'But I love him too.' Mary had come face to face with her central ambivalence, the contradiction of her *both* hating and loving him. By fully allowing the fury she felt there had been a dramatic switch into love and sadness. After the outburst she was very quiet and sad for what seemed like hours.

It was quite a new way of thinking for Mary, and for several weeks afterwards she would say to me: 'But how can you *both* love and hate someone at the same time?' During the same period she was also for the first time able to talk about the negative aspects of her parents. Mary admitted that perhaps they had been too strict, too rigid and that, yes, there had been a hierarchy in the family, with her at the bottom.

But the acceptance of ambivalence had also brought a deep sadness and sense of being alone. I agreed with her when she talked about being ultimately alone and how sad that was. It felt as if Mary had to mourn the ending of not only her belief in perfect parents and a perfect husband, but also the split in herself that had kept them all on a pedestal. When she blamed herself for everything and felt weak in contrast to their strength, she had been deeply dependent on them. The gap where her angry, strong self should have been was filled by a glue that stuck her to them.

As Mary accepted her angry, strong side more and more, she did not need her 'authority figures'. The 'glue' began to soften. She could become more of a separate person. But with that separateness came the sad sense of aloneness. We stayed with that sadness for a long time, but gradually out of it came a more solid sense of her new-found independence. It also felt frightening. It had been much easier to gear her life to what others wanted. She had become very clever at tuning in to other people's needs and interests. She used to use up a lot of energy working out what her husband was feeling, which was far from easy as he didn't show much affection. Only when she thought she knew how he felt, would she react. While reacting to him she didn't have to think about what *she* wanted or felt. Mary didn't even know what kind of music she really liked, as she had always listened to what he enjoyed.

Being 'alone' felt both exhilarating and scary. Who was this person called Mary? What did she really want out of life?

Louise

After one session when Louise had talked about feeling more powerful than her mother, she came back the next week looking very sheepish. She admitted to me that she was really embarrassed to have shown me the side of herself that did indeed feel superior. I asked her if she was afraid that she might feel more powerful than me. She denied this most emphatically, but at the end of the session she said that I did not look well, and asked if I was all right. In fact I did not feel or even look particularly ill that day, but Louise was so used to protecting other people that she didn't really trust me to be strong enough for her, that she was reacting to me in the same way. Was I strong enough to contain the angry feelings that were emerging?

It had seemed easier for Louise to reveal her vulnerable side than to show her powerful side to me. The two sides were still very split. She could talk about the side that felt responsible for the whole world and how she felt that everything would collapse unless she was in charge. Now Louise also recognized the child side that wanted to give up completely and be looked after by others. The child side was furious with all those people who she felt that she had to look after. But although she could understand the split with her intellect, she was still terribly afraid that the two sides could not possibly both be acceptable to the same person, for example, to me. Being vulnerable was acceptable in counselling, but being powerful was not acceptable, Louise feared. She worried that I wouldn't like her if she showed her powerful side. She was afraid that it might stir feelings of competition between us and she felt that she had to protect me from such feelings of competition, as she had protected her mother. For if she won the competition, then she would be without the support she depended on, as it seemed as though only someone much more powerful could be depended upon. She wanted to keep me 'up' on a pedestal.

Then one day Louise commented that I was much smaller physically than her. Apparently she was often envious of thin people. Was she envious of me? Yes, apparently she was rather envious. But no sooner had Louise admitted this feeling that she began talking about another friend of hers who was also thin. This friend was clearly dominated by Louise, who told me how much she resented the friend not 'pulling her weight' in the relationship. Louise was the one who always organized their outings. She may have been envious of thinness, but she also despised the apparent 'weakness' that she associated with being thin or small. It was hard at first to accept that she could both envy and despise thin people, including me.

When we looked at these feelings honestly together and talked about the difficulty of really feeling equal to another person, Louise relaxed visibly. We even joked and laughed about it, partly to discharge strong feelings, but also because there is something absurd about our culture's determination either to admire or to despise, either dominate or be dominated all the time. Could we really *both* be powerful, in our different ways? At that moment we were both deeply conscious of being together in the room, two powerful, but also vulnerable, human beings. There was an almost spiritual connection. We seemed really to face each other for the first time. We had connected on some deeper level by, as it were, 'leaping through the fire and envy and competition' to the other side. And we were both still in one piece at the end of the 'ordeal'. Now Louise could more comfortably accept her powerful side, knowing that it would not destroy me. I could still be there for her when she was feeling powerful as well as when she was vulnerable.

All three clients had come to some sense of acceptance of previously rejected sides of themselves. The next stage involves looking at what we *do* with this.

7 Making Changes: Living with the Opposites

> In the future elaboration of the new holistic world, the notion of rhythm is likely to play a very fundamental role.
>
> (Capra, 1982: 326)

In the last chapter we reached a middle or centre point in the process of counselling. We described this middle phase as coming to terms with the contradictions of life, of accepting ourselves as we actually are in the present. For some clients this kind of acceptance can take years, and the middle phase of counselling may only involve the acceptance of *one* previously denied aspect of the self, such as anger. Or it may involve losing *one* illusion, such as a feeling of childhood omnipotence.

The Rhythm of Life — Death and Rebirth

But for most clients this is a stage of loss as well as gain. It may involve the loss of believing that one is always 'nice' or always a 'victim' or totally 'in control'. As the client begins to accept the 'other' side too, so she loses the illusion of one-sidedness. She also loses the illusion of having the 'perfect' parent, friend, partner, counsellor, that so many of us have at some stage of our lives. It could be called a 'growing up' process in which we shed our childhood dreams. But reality and dreams are *both* needed for the processes of growth. It is not necessary or desirable to stop dreaming and imagining, but rather to *know* when we are working with dreams, images and symbols and when we are working with the reality of our daily lives. Problems exist when we think that the fantasy is real. The split between 'reality' and 'fantasy' or imagination, in which one is acceptable and the other isn't, is one of the many destructive and hierarchical splits of our patriarchal culture. We try to separate them, and subjugate one to the other, but fail. I try to work with *both* reality *and* imagination as equally valuable partners in adult life. Images can focus feelings in powerful ways to help us understand ourselves better.

One of the most powerful images for this middle stage of counselling is some kind of symbolic death. After all, the loss of the old illusions, or old patterns of seeing and being, is like a death of the old self into a new more accepting self. It is similar to the initiation ceremonies of some ancient cultures, most of which involve a separation from mother and/or childhood security, and then in some special place a series of rituals and tests are undergone, frequently ending in some kind of symbolic death and resurrection, such as leaping through fire or being covered up and then re-emerging.

Another useful set of images for this process are the changes of the ancient triple *moon* goddesses of virgin/mother/crone. The middle period involves going 'down' into previously hidden parts of the psyche. Often these are parts of ourselves that we symbolically describe as dark. These qualities, and death, were associated with the goddess in her form as old woman or crone, e.g. Hecate, who was the goddess connected with the centre of crossroads in ancient Greece. She is also associated with winter, when the previous harvest has been cut down and the new growth is still under the surface. Winter is also a time of holding in energy, of consolidating inner strength, before moving into spring, when it can be expressed outwardly.

Myths of death and rebirth are common throughout the ancient world, as we saw in Chapter 1. Initially the goddess herself would symbolically die and re-emerge, as in the Summerian myth of Innana. Then in more patriarchal societies it became the son who 'died' and was reborn in order for the crops to grow, for example Dionysius. There was generally a cyclical concept of recurring deaths and rebirths, and this concept is useful in counselling, as most clients go through the cycle many times in their spiral of growth. Each time they go through the middle stage at a different level. For example, in the first few sessions a client, who we will call June, realized that a side of her was very angry and that she wasn't the totally gentle, unselfish person that she thought she was. The loss of this picture of herself is like a small death for her. She may then re-emerge able to get much more strongly in touch with her needs and desires, and begin to live more assertively. She has accepted that she has a right to want affection, for example, from her rather undemonstrative husband. Anger is seen as an understandable response rather than something completely unacceptable and wicked. She accepts and gets used to her own anger rather than being frightened of it.

But a further stage of June's growth might involve getting some of her needs met by the counsellor, feeling safe and secure with her. This might involve seeing the counsellor as perfect and totally giving, so she would need to go through the whole process again, separating from the counsellor by disagreeing with her and even getting angry with her. June would then lose her illusion of the perfect carer and face a new death. Then she would re-emerge once again, a stronger, more whole person.

What may take one client a few sessions may take another several years. Some clients may have moved through several cycles of growth before coming to counselling. There can also be smaller cycles within 'bigger' ones. One whole small cycle can even be experienced in a one-day workshop designed to increase self-understanding. A person may come to terms with a previously hidden side, perhaps a part of herself that wants to boss everybody about. She would have to feel safe first in the group, then face up to the new knowledge and the loss of old image it involves. She may then learn new ways to express this new side constructively. she will then go on to new self-discoveries and new cycles.

In a sense these critical spiralling processes go on throughout our lives, whether we are having counselling or not. The counsellor can be seen as a kind of guide that people may need for certain parts of their ongoing journey. The guide may be needed at times of crisis, or when a person feels stuck or is making a change of direction, or when a re-evaluation of goals in life is needed. A guide can be especially helpful when a person is going through the middle phase of one cycle of their journey. For this is the phase involving 'going deeply' into the self, and can lead to depression and other psychological difficulties.

The feminist counsellor can help lead the client into new under-standings of herself and the influences that society has had on her, by showing her *how* to examine her own feelings and thoughts.

The Last Phase — Behaving Differently 'in the World'

This is the stage of re-emergence, or coming 'back into the world'. It is the stage when the client learns actually to express the newly accepted parts of herself. She learns to incorporate them into her everyday life. So the counsellor needs to use some problem-solving strategies, as at this stage the client often wants to make real changes to life-style or career or personal life. The counsellor first tends to use an exploratory strategy, as when a client is asked to write down all the pros and cons of a particular course of action, for example leaving a job. It may be necessary to redefine objectives at this stage and to help the client work with priorities. It is important to balance the reality-based, problem-solving strategies with the supportive strategies based on non-judgemental acceptance. For it often seems that at this stage the counsellor's own values are more likely to interfere with growth than at other times. The counsellor may often not agree with choices that the client makes. A feminist counsellor, for example, might be disappointed if a battered wife decides to return to a violent husband. Clients are still likely to be looking for the counsellor's approval in the choices that they make, unless they have reached a point where they are genuinely not influenced by the counsellor's values, or even if she doesn't want to please the counsellor any more, the client may still act in rebellion towards what she thinks her parents (or the counsellor) want her to do. Clients often project on to counsellors what their own 'conscience' or inner parent's voice is telling them. The counsellor needs continually to bring them back to what they *really* want or think for themselves.

During this stage some clients are learning for the first time since they were small children to listen to what their own voices are telling them. They may have their own contradictions and conflicts, but at least they are their own. However, it is surprising how often people find that when they do really listen to themselves they just seem to know intuitively what they should do.

When the new (or more accepting) being is emerging from the winter into the spring, she is often afraid and unused to expressing all parts of herself. She is like a bird emerging from the egg, who still has to learn to fly. It takes time to learn what can often be described as new skills for living.

Much support may be needed at this stage, not only to make decisions, but to live through their outcomes. A woman who decides to leave her husband and another one who decides to stay both need support to live with their choices. Often the counsellor will be involved in encouraging clients to find support for themselves outside the sessions if they don't already have it. The counsellor can suggest alternative ideas without being too directive; for example, if a woman has said herself that she would like support from another woman, the counsellor may suggest a few places or contacts to investigate.

At this stage there is often a strong sense of being two equal human beings working on some 'problems' together. There is more of an 'adult to adult' than 'parent to child' relationship. In a sense the client has 'grown up'. But there will still be times when she needs some parenting, so there can also sometimes be a 'parent to adult' relationship between counsellor and client. There are other times when the counsellor is acting in yet another role, as a teacher. She may, for example, feel that it is important to teach assertiveness skills (described in detail in the next chapter). She may feel the need to teach the client some relaxation skills, or some time and energy management skills. Exactly how these are practised is up to the client, but many useful techniques and frameworks can be shared when it seems appropriate.

The Rhythm Frameworks

Many clients talk about wanting a balance between the opposite sides of themselves that they are now conscious of. While the early stages of counselling involved separating out and discovering the opposites and the middle phase involved accepting them, the final phase involves balancing them in the rhythms of everyday life.

Emotional Rhythms
We cannot usually be both sides of ourselves at once. Thus, we can't be both angry and placatory at the same time. We try to do it when we are not fully conscious of our opposites, when we think we are being nice, but are so angry underneath that everyone gets confused messages. When someone feels comfortable with both sides of her nature she can experience her rhythms of anger and love consciously, rather than thinking she must *always* be nice. There are times to put others first and times to put oneself first or be selfish.

Rather more abstract opposites are those of acceptance and rejection of people, situations, or even ideas. You cannot accept and reject at the same time, but over time most of us do both, even to the same person or idea. A person who has been very one-sided, accepting everything, may find it difficult to reject anyone or anything even when she has realized that she does have a hidden rejecting side. Getting used to rejecting people's behaviour is especially hard for many women. It is often believed that if you reject someone's *action*, for example when a man is untidy at home or makes an unwanted advance, then you are rejecting the whole person. Learning to reject or criticize is an important skill for women to develop. Counsellors may need to show clients that it can be done without putting down the whole person. We all have a right to reject anything we don't like. For example, a suggestion that a family holiday be taken in a particular place was rejected by a wife who had always before gone along with her husband's wishes. It felt terrible to her at first actually to say to him, 'No, this year I don't want to go to France.'

It is often necessary to reject one idea before accepting another. So for women and men who are trying to express their wants and desires, being able to say 'No' to situations in which those needs are not met is often a first step. The woman who said 'No' to France was then able to express her desire to go to a particular other place. Rejection is only the other side of acceptance. They are both equally important in the rhythms of life.

Giving and receiving are two more rhythmically interconnected opposites that affect everyday life. Many people, especially women, because of our mothering role, are more used to giving and nurturing others than receiving for themselves. Many women clients find learning to receive the most difficult aspect to accept. When in company, even at other people's houses, many women will automatically get up and start bustling around taking care of everyone. It can be a useful way of hiding shyness, but it can also be connected to being afraid of receiving, perhaps because that makes a woman feel weak. For so long women's only major power has been that of giving and nurturing in the home. Learning to receive and be nurtured feels very vulnerable. They keep wanting to put their feet on the ground, somehow not quite trusting that the other person is capable of really giving as well as they are. In one couple the husband was not such a good cook as the wife, who always made the meals. But when she stopped cooking, he actually welcomed the opportunity to *give* for a change. He seemed to have been quietly resenting a situation in which he was always on the receiving end. Coming to counselling is one way in which a 'giver' can 'receive'. This may need to be pointed out by the counsellor.

However there are also clients who, perhaps because they had insufficient nurturing as babies, are always on the receiving end. They are forever looking for others to give to them, and yet often it is never enough. These people need to learn the opposite skill of giving. The counsellor can help by suggesting ways of giving. At first it might feel rather false. Perhaps presents are bought or meals are cooked without much feeling, but then as the client accepts the giving side of herself more and more, and learns to give herself more of the love and nurturing she lacked in childhood, it is likely that her rhythms of giving and receiving will flow more naturally. The counsellor is often nurturing her during sessions, but can also suggest ways in which she can nurture herself, for example, by giving herself treats like having a massage.

Although some of these behaviour changes appear to be rather superficial, they do seem to complement the 'deeper' changes that are going on in the unconscious as a client accepts herself more. By practising new behaviours the inner acceptance is also strengthened. Once again feminist counsellors do not think in terms of either/or, but rather in terms of both the behavioural level and the unconscious, psychodynamic level. They are both necessary, especially in this last stage of counselling. Inner acceptance makes the new behaviours easier, and acting 'as if' you accept a new side (e.g. a receiving side) helps you actually to accept it.

Relationship Rhythms

In healthy relationships there is a good rhythm between giving and receiving, both people playing both roles at different times. Yet in so many relationships even between friends, one person is dominant and generally in control, while the other one is relatively dependent or even submissive. This is the pattern of relating most acceptable and even thought of as 'natural' in patriarchal societies. And when one partner begins to change through having discovered their 'other side', the other one may not like it at all. A wife who stops being submissive and begins to demand more independence and to go out on her own more is rarely encouraged by her husband, who may have liked his dominant role. A woman may even feel that she has to choose between the relationship and her own growth. The counsellor may suggest that they both go to couple counselling, often a useful complement to individual work in such situations. But it is also important that the client keeps her own counsellor for herself, so that she runs no risk of being submerged within the couple again. The counsellor is always essentially on the client's side, but should not ever attack the partner who is unknown. The important thing is that the rhythms within the client are able to flow. She needs to be able to be in charge and dominant sometimes, and to let go and be de-pendent at other times. If the external situation makes this flow im-possible, then changes to that situation need to be looked at.

Rhythms of Control and Letting Go

Counsellors often have to encourage clients to find areas of their life where they can let go of the rigid control that so many people have over themselves and others. In the home it is often women who are in control. Many women are afraid of 'letting themselves or the house go', meaning that untidiness or dirt or lack of rigid organization must lead to the most unthinkable chaos. A counsellor might suggest that a client finds time during the week to wear comfortable clothes and no make-up, and to leave the washing-up. This could be seen as a kind of homework. Often counsellors suggest that clients give themselves special times each week for themselves and let others in the house-hold get on with their lives without them. The rhythm between control and letting go of control is one of the most difficult to learn. Often people are anxiously in control all the time, of themselves, or their homes, of work, of their children, of their partners, of the daily routine. And then when it has been one-sided for too long they swing into the extreme opposite and get drunk, fall into bed with a stranger or run away to Timbuctoo.

Underlying this rigid control is usually a deep fear, perhaps of being abandoned or of being worthless. This fear may have been faced in the middle phase of counselling, and the realization reached that we are ultimately alone and that our parents did and will some-times reject us. But the old habit of being in control is deeply ingrained in our everyday behaviour. To begin with, the counsellor may need to help the client to stop themselves consciously at certain points during the day and ask themselves whether they really need to perform a certain behaviour, such as tidying up. As they feel better about themselves, so will the need to present a perfectly controlled image, home, family to the world begin to lessen. Clients will also be more in touch with what they really feel and be able to develop their own values, standards, tastes and styles.

People who spend much of the day in jobs that demand a lot of control need to make an especially conscious effort to let go of control at other times. Sexual relations are a vital way of 'letting go', and often people with sexual difficulties also have problems with control. For women these difficulties may include quite justifiable responses to aggressive, invasive or continuously dominating sexual behaviour from a male partner. 'Letting go' physically and expressing sexual desire for many women is in reality threatening especially in heterosexual relationships. All too often it does lead to physical or mental pain and humiliation, inflicted by men whose sexuality is too intimately linked with aggression.

Yet the sexual arena can be a place where a rhythm between dominance and submission is played by both partners, but at different times. If both partners, whether heterosexual, gay or lesbian, can take turns at being relatively dominant, then *both* sides of each person are given expression. In our patriarchal culture the frequently sado-masochistic relationship, with one partner always dominant is more common. Many adults have only learnt one way of being sexual and may even have had childhood experiences of sexual attack and submission that set the pattern for later life.

Physical Rhythms

When the idea of rhythms and cycles is discussed, many clients refer to their menstrual or life cycles in describing current feelings. Because women menstruate we are more conscious of the cyclical nature of our feelings and energies. For example sexual energy tends for many women to be highest in the middle of the cycle (as this is usually the time for ovulation), and also around menstruation. Many clients talk about P.M.T. in sessions. So-called pre-menstrual tension is recognized by many feminists today as begin the time when a particular kind of powerful intuitive energy is available to women, and it tends to become aggressive only when not expressed. Menstruation is also often a time when energies flow inwards and women want to withdraw from the world to allow the empowering process to continue without outside interference. All of us, men as well as women, need to have times to let our energies flow inwards and other times when we need to let them flow outwards towards the world. After menstruation, women's energies tend to move outwards and it is a good time for starting new projects. Then after the peak in the middle, the energy moves back inwards and finally into the depths from which it then re-emerges.

The same basic patterns operate for most people in daily lives at various levels. Some clients find this a useful way of thinking about their cycles. In the modern Western world we have lost touch with this rhythmic way of living and do not organize our work lives around the model of rhythm as we need to in order to get the best out of both women and men. Everyone has their particular personal rhythms. Sometimes I suggest that clients notice for themselves what their own natural rhythms are. For example, one client's daily rhythms might involve increased energy at night and sluggishness in the mornings. Other clients peak in the afternoons. Most people seem to be able to work hard for fairly short stretches of time, e.g. one and a half hours, and then need a rest, even if only for a few minutes.

There are daily rhythms, weekly rhythms, monthly and even yearly rhythms. There are also the rhythms of whole lifetimes. For everyone there are times for resting and consolidating new experiences or insights, and times for going out and making changes. Middle age (whenever that is) is often seen by Jungian therapists as a time for consolidating and rethinking, often followed by a change perhaps even of career direction. But every phase of life has both its movement 'out', its 'peak' and its withdrawal of energy, and then its depth. Clients can be helped to recognize these cycles as they are happening and even to anticipate them in the future. Though it can be hard to change from a strictly one-directional, goal-orientated model to a more rhythmic one, the rhythm model can help clients to organize their lifestyles in ways that allow for all sides and all phases of their lives and energies.

Lifestyle Rhythms

For most of us, there are times when we need to be with other people and times when we need to be alone. (Being alone is different from being lonely, which is when we wish we were with others.) One client had a very crowded childhood in which there seemed to be little space for her; it was especially important for her to make time in her adult life for personal space. She said that she needed to live alone for a while, or at least to have a room in which she could be private when she needed to be. For her and for many women, especially those who are living with partners and/or families, it can feel strange at first to demand more personal space. As a feminist counsellor I try to support and validate this need when a client begins to feel it for herself. Couples are supposed to share everything, including rooms. Women are supposed to be always available for their children or partners, and it is culturally accepted that women's space can be invaded at any time. While children are often told 'not to disturb Daddy while he is working', Mother's door should always be open. Many women going through counselling decide that they need a room for themselves, or that they need to go away for a while alone. I try to encourage each client to find her own rhythm for being with others and being alone, rather than one imposed on them through cultural expectations and sex roles.

The idea of finding our own rhythms is especially important for women today, who are often faced with more choices than their grandmothers were. This gives us freedom, but with it comes enormous pressure from all directions telling us what we should do with our lives. I encourage clients to look at all the 'shoulds' in their lives. We should be superwomen, career women, perfect hostesses, exciting lovers, but we should also be perfect mothers, beautiful and slim, and so on. Balancing their *own* needs and energies is likely to be more satisfying and less stressful than keeping up with all the 'shoulds'. However, I have to watch my own 'shoulds' as a feminist counsellor. There can be feminist 'shoulds' as well as patriarchal 'shoulds', such as 'You *should* be a lesbian', or 'You *should* have a career', or 'You *should* never just stay at home with children.' Each person needs to find their own balance between their 'active' and 'resting' sides, their 'private' and 'public' sides, self-expression and caring for others.

Julia

During the middle phase Julia had become far more aware of her emotional needs and longings. She allowed herself to want things, like having children, that had not seemed important before, when she was stuck in her intellectual side. She was still not very comfortable in her physical being. This seemed to be a side that needed a lot more attention in order to redress the imbalance between body and mind. She herself suggested that some form of yoga or massage would help her to develop the 'body side'. And after a year of counselling Julia did sign up for a regular yoga class and also took up playing squash with a group of people she knew from univeristy. 'Squash helps let out some of that anger as well', she admitted half-jokingly.

Julia lived so much in her head that I also suggested some techniques for helping her be aware of her body throughout her daily life. One of these was to stop herself whenever she could, on the street or in the kitchen, in bed or at parties, and just notice that she was 'here', physically present. She could quietly say to herself 'I am here.' She could also notice her breathing and make the out-breaths take longer than the in-breaths, which is a relaxation technique. We tried out other 'grounding' exercises, including simply keeping her feet on the ground and being aware of their contact with the earth. We did some relaxation work that involved imagining warm energy rising from 'mother earth' through her feet and legs and into the rest of her body.

We also explored her feeling about herself as a woman and her unconscious denial of this reality. We focused a lot on her tummy and womb — centres of female power and creativity. Julia had felt initially that the 'feminine' side of life was weak, that only the 'masculine' really mattered and was powerful. So we looked at images of powerful women both in the present and the past, including some of the ancient goddesses. This exploration, which was somewhat intellectual, seemed to bring together her two sides. She was using mental analysis to develop a sense of her own physical and emotional power. Julia began to respect female power more and more as she talked with me and read and studied. At this point in the counselling I was often playing the role of teacher.

Julia also began drawing and crayoning in the sessions. At first I had asked her to draw different sides of herself and another time to draw herself and her family. Then she started drawing and painting at home and showing me what she had done. She also brought poems with vivid visual imagery. And then one day she came and announced to me that what she really wanted to do was to paint and to write. She didn't want to be an academic like her parents.

We then began exploring ways in which she might put her new wants into practice. Julia began discussing with friends the possibility of buying a place in the country. She began looking at ways of earning enough money to live on, even considering going on social security for a while. Although she still did not have a satisfactory sexual relationship, she was becoming more relaxed with men. And although the possibility of having children seemed a long way off, she was actually beginning to give birth to herself and to her hidden creativity. Julia did in fact have several dreams at this point about giving birth. She understood very clearly for herself what the symbolism of these dreams meant for her, without me interpreting them.

Mary

In the middle phase Mary had come to terms with the sense of being ultimately alone. She could no longer look to others for confirmation of her existence in the way that she used to. Her question now was 'Who am I?' In order to get to know her *own* needs, interests and natural rhythms, Mary felt that she needed more space. After exploring various practical possibilities, she decided that she had to have one room in their house that was all her own. She needed to be able to lock the door and only let people in when she chose to. Mary felt that she badly needed space for herself. Even as a child she had always shared rooms with sisters. Her husband seemed to understand at first, but became increasingly sulky, and Mary needed a lot of support to go through with this change of lifestyle. Fortunately she had one close woman friend who was very supportive, and we also looked at the possibilities of women's groups and classes in her local area. Mary found a centre for women, and although there were no 'consciousness-raising' groups at that time, she did enrol for self-defence classes where she met other supportive women. It also helped her to feel less terrified of going against her husband's wishes. He had never actually hit her, but Mary seemed to be afraid that one day he might.

Mary did eventually move into her own room, and she negotiated for her and her husband to spend alternate nights in each other's rooms. This was a big step for her. She kept wanting to change her mind, every time her husband sulked about anything in the house. She felt guilty, as though it was because she had moved into her own room that he was upset. She had to keep being reminded by me and others that she had a right to her own space. With Mary in this final stage of counselling I had played both the role of 'problem-solving helper' when we looked at how she could make space for herself and then that of 'teacher' and 'supporter' when she was actually carrying through the decisions that she had made.

Louise

Louise was so used to being 'in charge' all the time that the opposite of letting others take care of her felt very difficult. She had been able to practice this 'other side' in the counselling sessions. But now she said that she wanted to try out new behaviour outside the sessions. Firstly she felt that she needed more 'treats' that didn't necessarily involve food. We did some problem-solving work together on practical ways that she could 'treat' herself and be looked after. Louise decided to have massage once a week. She also decided to make outings with her women friends a regular part of her weekly rhythms. As Louise no longer wanted to be always the dominant one with friends, she asked if they could decide where they wanted to go in turns. So one week it was Louise's turn, the next it was Sue's turn, and on the third week it was Annette's. Louise also started accepting invitations to go to their houses and be in situations where she was the guest and being looked after. At first it had felt strange and she had wanted to jump up and offer to help in the kitchen every five minutes. But her friends seemed to enjoy the new pattern and would 'make' her sit down.

Louise was also getting increasingly impatient with her husband, who she felt was 'just like a little boy'. She was fed up with playing mother to him all the time. She stopped having meals ready for him when he came home from work. He started complaining and criticizing her for not being a 'proper wife'. Louise was hurt by these accusations, but was so determined to develop her own independence that his resentment did not stop her from going out and being more relaxed about meal-times. We even talked about finding ways of letting go and not being tidy and clean all the time. Louise herself came up with the idea of having Sunday as her 'day off' and asking Tom to cook the lunch. This seemed to work very well at first, but the guilt did not go away. Louise started to help Tom with the Sunday lunch and after a few weeks reverted to old patterns.

One day Louise came to a session looking rather scared and dishevelled. She told me that Tom had been drunk the night before and after shouting abuse at her, he had finally hit her. She had told him she was leaving and had packed her bags there and then and driven over to her mother's. She hadn't slept all night and wondered what should she do. Louise sat there looking for advice, tearful but defiant. At first I just stayed with her while she cried and raged against him. Then she began to talk about her need for him and her fear of independence. Underneath there was still a frightened little girl. The thought of living alone was far more scary than the thought of living with a demanding and abusive 'little boy' husband. At the end of the session she looked more cheerful and told me that now she had decided to go back home. 'Thank you for your help', she said. Then out she walked. I had hardly spoken a word for the whole session. My role had been that of a supporter in crisis and of a container for her own decision-making process. All I did was simply to *be there*.

In later sessions Louise and I did some problem-solving work on her relationship with Tom. She wrote down 'good' and 'bad' things about him and about the relationship and the pros and cons of leaving him and staying together. Eventually Louise decided to stay with him and worked out for herself the losses and sacrifices as well as the gains in her decision. At least the choice had been made by Louise in the light of her own self-understanding. She also realized that there was still a lot of work to do on strengthening her own deeper sense of independence and on improving communication between herself and Tom.

For Louise, as for the two other clients, there was a need to develop and practise assertiveness skills and attitudes to provide a sense of genuine inner power, and to communicate needs clearly and in an equal way to others. In the next chapter we explore the usefulness of assertiveness training for women and men.

8 Assertiveness Training: Expressing the Opposites

Assertive power is a power of equality
and being direct about that equality.

(Dickson, 1982: 151)

In order to put new behaviours or lifestyle changes into practice many clients need to learn to be more assertive. Many women especially have been used to being passive and giving, and sometimes exploding with frustrated aggression it is hard for them to learn a middle way of communicating to others. Being assertive is not the same as being aggressive; it doesn't mean putting others down instead of letting them put you down. It is essentially a way of communicating one's needs clearly to others and asking for some concrete change that may then be negotiated. It involves respecting oneself *and* the other person and their needs, first being clear about exactly what you want and then standing your ground, even if you don't get what you want. At the very least you feel more self-respect when you ask clearly and honestly than when you give up completely, or get aggressive, or ask only indirectly. Assertiveness is direct, honest, clear communication between equally valued human beings. It is the opposite of the normal form of communciation in our patriarchal society, which is mainly between superiors and inferiors, with one person 'on top' and the other 'below'.

People are usually passive, aggressive or manipulative in hierar-chical communication situations. The same person may be all three at different times. For example a woman might be very passive with her husband but take out her frustration and resentment on her children. With them she is aggressive. And when she wants something from her husband she has to use subtle, manipulative methods to get it. Many women have learnt that indirect manipulation is the only way to get their needs met. If she wants him to go out with her more often, she might start sulking and complaining that she is bored on Saturdays, while an assertive woman would tell him clearly how she felt and what she wanted, with a concrete suggestion for change. She might say: 'I realize that you have a lot of extra work at the moment' (respecting his needs) 'but I feel sad that we don't go out together at all these days, and would like to go out on Saturday. I'd like to see the new movie that's on down the road next Saturday. I've checked that there are seats available for the 7.30 show.'

Some people are really aggressive a lot of the time, and others might think 'She doesn't need any assertion training.' But aggression is not the same as assertion. It is often a reaction to situations, maybe even in childhood, where people have themselves been put down and suffered aggressive or even violent treatment at the hands of others. As we live in such a hierarchical and often violent (in subtle as well as obvious ways) society, it isn't surprising that most people swing between aggression and passivity for most of their lives.

A good image for this stage in the cycle is that of the virgin goddess part of the ancient triple goddess, for example Artemis. The original meaning of the word 'virgin' in both Latin and Greek meant 'whole woman who belongs to no man'. As Nor Hall writes, 'Virgin means one-in-herself; not maiden inviolate, but maiden alone, in-herself . . . The virgin acts according to her own nature; she may give herself to many lovers but like the moon, she can never be possessed' (Hall, 1980: 11). In order to be assertive and have a strong sense of separate self, women need to think of themselves as 'women unto themselves, belonging to no one ultimately but themselves'. There is also a sense in which the 'virgin' is in closer contact with nature and with the instincts, as implied by expressions such as 'virgin territory'. This ability to be in touch with feelings and with the body is a vital part of feminist (and most other kinds of) counselling. It is a great strength and has enormous healing power. And yet in patriarchal society there is a deep fear of female instinctual energy that is not squashed into domestic boxes and controlled and possessed by men. Being assertive does not actually involve a completely 'wild, uncontrollable, devouring' approach to other people. It respects the other and has its own rules and boundaries. And yet society's fear of assertive women betrays a much deeper fear of female power. In women, assertiveness is often labelled 'aggression' by men and even by some women. Nevertheless, assertive communication is a vital model for the future, if we wish to create a society where mutual understanding and respect are the norm.

The counsellor who continually brings a client back to herself when she has been busy talking about everyone else is using assertiveness. The counsellor who suggests that a client could use the word 'I' when she has been talking in terms of 'one' or 'people' is training in assertiveness. The counsellor who says 'But what do *you* want?' when a client keeps talking about her husband's needs, is training in assertiveness. And counsellors can also convey some of the more specific techniques involved.

Assertive Techniques

Asking Clearly for a Change

This basic assertion skill is usually practised first in role-playing situations suggested by the trainer or counsellor. I might suggest that the
client practises asking for cold soup to be changed in a restaurant, or
asking someone to stop smoking in a non-smoking part of a cinema.
Counsellors generally start with fairly non-threatening situations with
strangers, and then move on later to more difficult situations involving personal relationships or work settings. Sometimes it is helpful to
act out passive, aggressive and indirect or manipulative approaches
as well. This helps a client feel, in her own body, the differences
between the four styles of communication. She might feel the frustration and powerlessness of passively accepting cold soup or irritating
cigarette smoke. And her body language is likely to be passive too.
She might lean forward in a placatory stance or smile too much. The
counsellor could herself act out the passive style to show her, or it
may be enough to point out how she is sitting. The counsellor may
suggest that she exaggerates the body language to get the point
across. When acting in the aggressive style some clients discover
untapped sources of anger that role-playing gives them the opportunity to express. It is often easier for clients to express difficult feelings
when 'hiding' behind a role.

But the most important part of this basic training is practising the
assertive style. One can often use a situation from 'real life' that a
client has brought to the session. For example, one woman was
having difficulties at work with a boss who assumed that she would
stay late whenever he needed her to. This particular woman had,
through counselling, recognized and accepted the side of her that was
really angry and felt exploited. She had written down furious feelings
towards her parents and raged about them with me. She had even
been able to share her resentment towards me for going on holiday.
Recently she had begun to talk about her boss and her anger towards
him. While it was difficult for her to make significant changes to her
behaviour with her actual parents, who were both very ill, she *could*
change her behaviour with the boss. So I explained to her the main
elements of assertion, stressing the importance of respecting the
other. Now that she had recognized her anger towards him she could
see his other side, which was very insecure. But most importantly she
could see him as an essentially equal human being. He was no longer
some kind of god. As she felt better about herself, so she could see
him more realistically, without either putting him on a pedestal or
putting him down. I shared some techniques that help people to bring

others off unrealistic pedestals, such as imagining them as babies having their nappies changed. The essence of assertion is equality, and in our society it is very hard really to feel equal to others. For this client, seeing others as equal also meant that she was neither super-special nor a complete 'nothing'. She was able to feel more 'ordinary', so she could also see her boss as more 'ordinary'. Women often put men on pedestals because they are still unconsciously seen by both sexes as more important than women.

This client had to go through the process of accepting her anger, increasing her self-esteem and seeing others as more ordinary and equal, before reaching the stage of changing her behaviour. So when it came to practising being assertive with her boss, she felt inside that she had a right to define her own boundaries and that he was not a terrifying all-powerful god figure.

I pretended to be the boss and we acted out her coming into the office and first asking for time to talk. I pretended to be carrying on with my work, almost ignoring her. She kept repeating 'I need to talk to you', but her voice was rather quiet. So I suggested that she tried talking louder, and we practised the first part again. I also pointed out that she was looking down and hunching her shoulders up. So she practised holding her head up higher and looking me in the eye.

When the body language showed more confidence, I (as the boss) gave her space to talk to me. She started apologetically: 'I'm sorry but . . .'. Afterwards I suggested that she didn't use the word 'sorry', and we worked out a 'script' together. 'I realise that you have a lot of pressure at the moment, but I feel taken for granted when you assume that I can stay after 5.30. Next time you need me to stay late, I would like you to ask me in the morning, so that I can tell you whether it is possible or not. Otherwise I shall leave at 5.30 every evening.' At first she found it hard to stick to the script. She went on talking about her various commitments after work as if making excuses for what felt like unreasonable behaviour. I had to point out to her that she had a right to stick to her own boundaries and that her contract actually said 9.30 to 5.30. Her fear was that she was being hard and cold, not sympathetic enough to her boss's needs. This feeling is common with women learning to be assertive. They have a horror of setting firm boundaries, as women have been so used to merging with others and losing a sense of themselves as separate beings. Boss–secretary relations often mirror those of traditional husband–wife, where the secretary feels more responsible for the boss's needs than for her own, especially where the boss is a man. There is also a lot of pressure on women to be caring and giving. Stating clear personal boundaries can be seen as non-caring, while in fact it is often better for the other person to know clearly where he or she stands, rather than always making assumptions about this.

I had to remind this client that she did not have to make excuses for her request. Then, as the boss, I pretended to argue with her, giving reasons why her request was not fair, and explaining how difficult things were at the moment. I pretended to play to her caring, sympathetic side. Once we got into an argument she began to lose ground and retreat. So I suggested that we start again, and she simply repeated the main sentences that we had agreed on and said nothing else. This technique is called the 'broken record'.

The Broken Record Technique

This technique is very useful when people need help in standing their ground and not getting caught up in arguments in which they feel they have to justify themselves. It involves simply repeating one or two significant sentences, such as, 'No, I'm afraid I can't come tonight' or 'I want you to listen to me.' If the other person realizes that they cannot change the speaker's mind, they usually accept what is being said. Once again this can feel very hard and cold for women not used to such firm forms of communication. But it does not necessarily involve putting the other person down. It is merely stating boundaries, like a bird or animal might define its territory. It is also important to stay calm while stating one's boundaries. Some deep breathing before making the statement might help.

Then, once the message has been heard, negotiation is possible. But for many women, being properly listened to and having their boundaries accepted has been so hard that they often need quite drastic measures to ensure that their message has really been heard and accepted. So every time the other person puts forward an argument, as when the boss tells my client how much he needs her support, she simply repeats the sentence 'I cannot stay after 5.30 today.'

Another client was so afraid of losing confidence in a real situation with her boss that she actually wrote down what she wanted to say on a piece of paper. She then told me that she had the piece of paper on her desk at work while talking to her boss. The paper helped to distance her from the other person whom she had had a habit of always rescuing.

Taking Time

Stepping outside the situation to decide what you want is another useful techniqe to employ when one is being asked to do something that one is not sure about. Women especially are trained to say 'yes' more than to say 'no'. They are expected to please others, passively accept what others want them to do, and be always available. Saying 'No' is often felt by women to be hard and cold, uncaring and even 'unfeminine'. But we often then feel resentful because we have agreed to do something that we didn't really want to do in the first place. One client was always agreeing to babysit with her friend's children as she had no children of her own, and felt that if she said 'No' it would be selfish. When her friend rang to ask her if she could babysit, she would automatically say 'Yes' without giving herself time to think about it. Later she would often regret it.

I told her that she had a right not to say 'Yes' straight away, but to ask for time to think about it. Then she could work out for herself whether it was convenient or not. She might end up still saying 'Yes', but at least she would not have taken the decision under the pressure of the moment.

Being assertive does not mean *always* saying 'No', or never putting other people's needs first. It means deciding for ourselves what course of action we want and then sticking to our request. When it is appropriate we might sometimes be passive or even aggressive, as when, for example, a man is sexually harassing us. But at least the choice is ours. We are communicating from the whole, separate self, after making a decision that we want to take a certain course of action.

In patriarchy it is a cliché that women say 'No' when they really mean 'Yes'. Women are thought of as always changing their minds, while men are supposed to be firm and decisive. This gender split is damaging to both men and women, who both need times when they can stand firm and say 'No' and times when they can 'flow' with the demands of the situation and not stand apart. The 'firm' kind of assertiveness is associated in our culture with the 'masculine' side of life. Men find it more difficult to achieve the other kind of assertiveness that involves accepting that *both* sides of an argument may be equally valuable and that *both* people or both sides are equally worthy of respect. Women's upbringing helps us to see both sides of situations and to empathize with others, but this makes it harder for us in those situations where we have to choose between action A or B, or between our needs and those of another person.

The culture has been split between 'masculine' and 'feminine' and individuals have learnt to emphasize one style OR the other. Yet simply for survival in the world, let alone self-expression, we all need both styles. We sometimes need to focus in one area of work or home and say 'No' to others ('masculine' mode), and at other times we need to see the connections between areas ('feminine' mode). People of either sex can learn skills involved in the side that has not been developed. These are not inborn styles of thinking and responding, they are learnt. Assertion training depends on the belief that anyone, however passive initially, can learn to be more assertive.

Sexual Assertiveness

One area where gender differences in assertiveness are especially noticeable is sexuality. Because Western culture has emphasized the passive role of women and the active role of men in sexual relationships, it is often particularly difficult for women to be assertive about their sexual needs. Sexual pleasure and desire is generally defined in male terms. The elements of conquest, penetration and orgasm, in that order, are seen as the main elements of sexual enjoyment. Male desire is increased by visual stimulation to a considerable extent, with bits of female bodies, separated from the whole, seen as the main 'turn-ons'. It is hardly surprising that women easily become obsessed with various bits of their bodies, such as breasts or bottoms.

One client came for counselling about difficulties in a heterosexual relationship with a man she had lived with for five years. It transpired that he received most of his sexual stimulation from pornographic magazines, which he would leave around the flat. Although their sexual relationship had initially been good, it had now deteriorated and they only made love about once a month, which my client felt was all her fault. She told me that she felt that she was not sexually attractive enough for him. We explored her feelings of inadequacy and at one point she began to cry. She told me that when all dressed up she often felt really attractive, and then the boyfriend would make some comment that criticized an aspect of her body or clothes, leaving her feeling completely deflated. Her eyes flashed as she spoke, so I said: 'You seem to be really angry with him.' She looked at me in surprise and then suddenly laughed a rather bitter laugh. 'Yes, you're dead right, I am.' Then she launched into a long tirade about the porno magazines. Later I said: 'It seems to me that you have been blaming yourself for this situation, whereas now I can see that you feel he has some responsibility too.' I then asked her what she would like to change. The question of changing could not usefully have come up until she had stopped totally blaming herself and put more of the 'blame' on to her partner. The first thing she wanted was for him to stop leaving his porno magazines around the flat. They made her feel uncomfortable and inadequate. Then she wanted to increase her own confidence in her sexuality. She told me that neither of them wanted to finish the relationship, she wanted it to develop into a more equal relationship. At present she felt dominated by him. In general, she wanted to become more assertive.

It seemed that a useful first step would be to ask him to put away the porno magazines. So I suggested that we practise talking to him about this issue. We pretended that he was sitting in a chair that I placed opposite her. I stressed the importance of respecting the other person but sticking determinedly to what she wanted to say, the essence of which was that the magazines made her feel uncomfortable and could he put them away and not leave them around the flat. She had a very concrete request, which is a good powerful start for using assertiveness. I told her about the broken tecord technique and suggested that she could, if necessary, keep repeating 'I want you to put them away.' At first the acting felt strange. She giggled a lot, but eventually managed to say her script to the chair in a serious, assertive way.

She did actually speak to him about the magazines the evening after she had been to see me. Apparently he laughed at her and called her a prude, but she insisted, and he did put them away. However it made her feel inadequate again, so for the next few sessions we looked at why she felt inadequate in terms of both his unreasonable criticisms and her own poor self-image and childhood experiences. Both factors were important. I also commented that she seemed a very sexual person to me. This too surprised her, and we had a discussion about sexuality not just being a way of attracting men, but about the whole way that we are in the world with all kinds of people, not just with sexual partners.

Later on she felt enough trust in me to share some of her own sexual fantasies, which proved to be quite a breakthrough in counselling. She was able to feel comfortable about her own sexual desires and interests being different and separate from her partner's. Previously she had only been involved in his fantasies, not even daring to admit that she had some of her own. Once she was in touch with her own sexual needs it would be much easier to be assertive about them to a partner. Unfortunately she stopped coming before we reached this stage, and I wondered whether the counselling was becoming too threatening for the relationship. She may have been afraid that if she continued she would end up leaving her boyfriend, and she chose to stay with him.

The Counsellor's Role

The counsellor is quite directive in assertion training and has to be careful not to become too dominating at this stage. It is important to use the client's own words when working out together what to say to a person the client needs to be assertive with. The emphasis needs to be on actions outside the sessions. The counsellor is not a judge or examiner either, so if a client fails to be as assertive as she had hoped, she won't be criticized. The counsellor might even affirm the difficulty of the task in our present patriarchal culture. But some achievements are vital, so the counsellor might suggest an easy task to begin with, such as making one phone call for a job application, or giving oneself a treat.

Practice is very important. The counsellor can assure her client that assertiveness gets easier and more 'natural' the more she practises, and that there will be times and situations in which it is more difficult than others. She might suggest that the client makes a list of situations, varying from 'easy' at the top to 'really difficult' at the bottom. The client can start with being assertive in the easier situations and then proceed to the more difficult ones later. Some people can be very assertive at work, but crumble with their children or partners. Others can be very assertive at home but are easily intimidated by authority elsewhere. Most people, even the most apparently confident, have one or two areas in their life where they need to be more assertive, and in counselling these will probably become clear.

Julia

Julia wanted at first to make really dramatic changes to her life, such as to go off to the country and paint. We spent some time during this final phase looking at her present situation and at what small and achieveable changes she could make. Because Julia had lived so much in her head, she often had wild fantasies that were too difficult to achieve in reality. When she failed to live up to the fantasies, she became depressed.

The first step we agreed was for her to make a certain amount of time each week for painting and for writing. Julia needed to be very firm about this and create what felt like quite rigid boundaries for herself. She had to focus on A and ignore B (e.g. friends). Then there was the question of relationships. One of the problems that had brought Julia to counselling was the generally unsatisfactory nature of her relationships with men. It seemed that she related to them through her head, seeking approval for her intellect as she had sought her father's approval. While she felt uncomfortable in her body, Julia did not even imagine that they could be attracted to her physically. The thought was too horrible and frightening. But as she began to feel more in touch with her body she began looking at herself with no clothes on in the mirror. At one stage I suggested that she spent some time each week massaging her tummy, which she felt particularly bad about.

Julia did have some close women friends with whom she spent a lot of time. She began to talk to them more and more openly about relationships and sex. She even tried masturbating for the first time, after talking about it with her friends. Some of the women Julia mixed with were lesbian and politically separatist, and one of them whom Julia admired intellectually, began to show a sexual interest in her. Julia was upset, and yet didn't want to appear 'not right on' or 'anti-lesbian'. In the following session we spent some time exploring Julia's own feelings about lesbians and about her own sexual and/or loving feelings towards women. I secretly hoped that she would be able to have this lesbian relationship, as I felt that it could be a healing relationship for her. Perhaps through an intimate relationship with another woman she would be better able to reclaim pride in her own body and its femaleness. As a counsellor, though, I kept this view to myself.

Julia decided that she did not want a sexual relationship with this friend at the moment, so then we looked at how she could be assertive in her response to the woman without showing disrespect for her in any way. We worked out three main sentences for her to say if the invitation came up again. Julia practised them, with me pretending to be her friend. At first she was really embarrassed and looked down all the time. Eventually I persuaded her to look me in the eye, and sit up straight while telling me that she didn't want a sexual relationship at the moment.

Julia was able to tell her friend how she felt, and was surprised how easily her feelings were accepted. The next time she came for counselling, Julia said that the assertion training had made her feel more confident about saying 'No' in other situations as well, but she still found it difficult to be on the other side, being the one to ask, or the one with the desires and needs. She was so scared of rejection. So we decided to make a list of easy to difficult requests that she might want to make. These ranged from inviting a new woman friend round to her flat for a meal, to asking a man to go to bed with her. She couldn't imagine that she would ever dare make such a suggestion to a man, in case he said 'No', so I pointed out that even if her suggestion was refused, it was not the *whole* of her that was being rejected. Just as Julia had refused her friend's request to sleep with her, but still wanted to be friends and continued to respect her, so one refusal does not mean a total rejection of a person as unworthy and unlovable. It would be the particular action that particular day that was being refused. And the more Julia risked rejection, the less threatening such risks were likely to feel. It would get easier as she practised more and more, starting with the less threatening social requests. We also talked about positive thinking, and the need to assume a 'Yes' response until the other person actually refuses, rather than starting off assuming that they will say 'No'.

Mary

Mary needed a lot of assertiveness training to negotiate with her husband over having a room of her own. She used the 'broken record' technique of repeating her request over and over again. Eventually her husband realized that she was determined and meant what she said, but Mary still felt very guilty. Much of this guilt began to be focused on James, their little boy of 3. She was afraid that by setting clear boundaries for herself and stating her own wants, she was being a bad mother. She found herself giving in to his demands more and more, until it became very difficult for her to say 'No' to him.

In the sessions we spent some time looking at what Mary thought a 'good mother' was, and how she seemed to have impossibly high expectations of herself. She also told me that her husband was always criticizing her for 'spoiling' James. For example, she would always stay with the child until he fell asleep, even if she fell asleep herself. While in one area of life she was being clearer about her boundaries and sense of being a separate self, she was finding it harder to separate from her son.

It seemed to be important for Mary to stop feeling guilty for not being the perfect mother. No one can actually be 'the perfect mother', despite all the advertising and social presures. Working with children herself made her even more conscious of the heavy social expectations. She did begin to recognize the unreasonableness of many of the conflicting demands made on her, and this helped Mary to feel less guilty, but she still felt that she needed to learn to be more assertive with James. Mary was afraid that she would 'smother' him in the way that she herself had felt 'smothered', but she empathized very closely with his every feeling.

First Mary had to achieve a sense of being a separate person from James. He had his own characteristics and journey of life, just as she had hers. I read to her the poem by Kahlil Gibran (1972) that starts with 'Your children are not your children, they are the result of life's longing for itself . . .' She liked the poem and said later that it had made her think. 'I realize that I have been over-identifying with James', she said when returning for the next session. I reminded her how successfully she had separated from both me and her husband, to become her own person. Then we wrote down all the ways in which her son was different from her, and ways in which he was the same. The 'different' list was much longer.

Then I asked her what changes she would like to make in her

relationship with him. She said that she would like to be able to say 'No' without feeling guilty. I asked what particular things would she like to say 'No' to, suggesting that she make these as detailed and concrete as possible. She produced a list for the next session, that included saying 'No' to demands for particular items in shops, requests for toys that other children had, requests for her to play with him when she was doing something else, requests for special foods when everyone was eating something else. And finally the most difficult situation of all, which for her turned out to be bedtimes. Mary herself had been afraid of the dark and never remembered sleeping alone. And yet putting James to bed was taking up a lot of precious time that she needed for herself.

We agreed that she would start with the easier 'No's' such as 'No' to sweets in the shop. She would simply keep repeating the sentence 'No, sweets are bad for you.' Even if James lost his temper or refused to leave the shop, Mary would stand her ground and repeat the phrase. She tried it out the following week and it worked, but she found it difficult not to answer his endless 'Why?'s. It seemed unreasonable not to explain more. I told her that she had a right as his parent to say 'No' while still respecting him. With Mary it was always vital to stress her need to respect herself as well as the other person. By being over-concerned with James' needs, and as a liberal parent respecting him as a person, she had actually been disrespecting herself.

Louise

Louise appeared on the surface to be very assertive. She was so often in powerful or controlling roles. But in fact she found it very difficult to assert her own *emotional* needs. She admitted to me that asking someone else to help her made her feel ashamed, as if her very need was a weakness. I asked her to look at situations in which she had felt a need and wanted to ask for help, but hadn't been able to. She told me that when she had left Tom the night when he had hit her, she had wanted to talk to her mother about the hurt she felt, but she hadn't been able to ask, as her mother would have blamed her. I asked what exactly it was that she would have liked her mother to say or do. It turned out that what she really wanted was for her mother to listen to her without judging her. I wondered whether it would be possible for Louise assertively to ask her mother for some time just to listen.

Even if Louise's mother was incapable of listening without judging, at least Louise had clarified what it was she wanted from her. And if Louise could say to her mother what she wanted to, it would make her feel more self-respect. We worked out some words that included a recognition of her mother's own needs. Her mother had been brought up to feel not good enough herself, and so hoped that her daughter would make up for her own inadequacies. When Louise turned out to be human and not perfect, she had been doubly disappointed. She had never thought that Tom was 'good enough' for Louise, so Louise's assertive communication began with the sentence 'I know that you don't think I should have married Tom, but I feel really terrible right now and I'd like you to listen to me for half a hour without telling me what you think.' When Louise did actually try this approach out on her mother, she was amazed to find that she understood and agreed just to listen. But after five minutes she couldn't resist interrupting with her own observations! Louise stood her ground and repeated: 'I just need you to listen, Mum.'

After that encounter with her mother, Louise felt that it would be easier to be assertive with friends who always told her their problems, without ever listening to hers. She told one friend 'Now you can listen to me. I've got a problem too.' Even admitting to having problems was hard for Louise, but she was having such a difficult time in her marriage that she needed to talk to her friends about what was going on. Gradually her friends got more used to her 'having a good old moan' with them.

While her assertiveness with friends and even with her mother improved, Louise found it almost impossible to be assertive with Tom. She still looked up to him at some level, just because he was a man. She was also a little afraid of him, and when in his presence she soon slipped back into the 'inferior wife' role. She admitted to me that it was just too hard to change. The only solution was to leave, and she couldn't do that.

I didn't feel that counselling had 'failed' with Louise just because she was still in a bad, but quite traditional, marriage. For all three clients, including Louise, important internal and some external changes of lifestyle had taken place. They all seemed to be more accepting of themselves as whole people, with the right to make demands on others, ready to stand on their own two feet.

There are many assertiveness training courses now available in adult education centres. Trainee and practising counsellors would benefit from experiencing such courses for themselves before applying the techniques with individual clients.

9 Standing Up on Both Feet: Endings and New Beginnings

> We have eaten of the fruit of Persephone and we are changed. We can never be wholly severed from the dark, the earth, the flesh.
>
> (Starhawk, *Dreaming the Dark*, 1982)

In the last chapter we looked at some techniques for helping clients to become more assertive in their lives. The emphasis was on actual, concrete changes to their lives and/or relationships outside the counselling sessions. In this chapter we come back to the counselling relationship and consider when and how to end it.

Sometimes there is a 'natural' end, such as when a client moves away or starts a new job. Or it may be clear to both client and counsellor that the changes created in the client's life have meant that counselling is no longer necessary. It may be that the symptoms that the client came with have disappeared: she has stopped obsessively washing her hands or compulsively eating. The conflict that she came with may have been resolved: a choice may have been made, for example between staying with or leaving a job or relationship. In some cases the counsellor and client may have decided months earlier on a time to stop. Many clients feel more comfortable with a pre-arranged duration of counselling of say three or six months or a year, although these deadlines can of course be adjusted. As many feminist counsellors work with people who do not have much money, a set number of sessions can be helpful for those with limited funds.

For many people the question about when to end counselling is not so simple. We have already noted that the process of psychological growth and change goes on throughout our lifetimes, and each cycle of counselling can be seen as part of an ongoing spiral. While each time there may be new insights, new acceptance of hidden parts of the self and new changes to lifestyle, the same themes and issues are likely to re-emerge later on. Or when one conflict is resolved, a new one comes to take its place. In a very real sense the counselling process never ends.

But what does end is the particular counselling relationship with one particular counsellor; and a real separation and parting from another human being does take place. It can feel like a kind of death; and how the two people work with that ending, and how the client experiences it, can be very important. For endings, losses and separations are part of everyday life, and it may be that the client has even come into counselling because she could not handle such partings well in the past. There may have been abrupt and painful separations from parents, or deaths. The client may have a terror of abandonment.

The difficulties clients may have with partings can be expressed according to their more general patterns of coping with difficult situations. Some clients tend to withdraw from pain and may be so afraid of rejection that they may leave early or just not turn up one day, rather than face a 'proper' goodbye. This may help them to feel more in control of the relationship. There may be others whose general pattern is to attack what feels painful. They are likely to complain that the counselling is useless and they aren't coming any more because 'it's all a load of rubbish'. Other groups of clients solve problems of separation by trying to merge with the other, to avoid feeling separate and therefore alone. They will cling on for as long as possible, always trying to please the counsellor. They will also be afraid of leaving in case it hurts the counsellor's feelings. They might be very passive and wait until the counsellor says it is time to finish.

Usually while these patterns are continuing, the client has not yet been through the middle phase of counselling when she has separated from the 'mother' and really faced herself, including some parts of herself she had not previously accepted. So many people have difficulties around separation especially from mothers, that they may need to go through several cycles of separation, self-acceptance and changing lifestyles before they feel really separate. So for clients in the initial cycles of counselling, it can be important just to notice their habitual patterns of dealing with endings, while at the same time it is necessary to present them with a more rhythmical feminist model of parting.

A Feminist Approach to Endings and Parting

The Rhythms of Life and Death
The feminist concept of life has a very different image of death and endings from the prevailing patriarchal one. In the modern world, death is seen as a final end, to be feared and overcome somehow. If you are a good Christian you go to heaven and *overcome* death that way. If you are a creative person you leave a monument or a work of art behind you. If you are a parent you produce children who will live after your death. In these ways you too think that you *overcome* death. But always the emphasis is on *conquering* or overcoming

death. It has to be fought against, defeated. And since it can't be, we often try to ignore it or 'sweep it under the carpet'. One way of dealing with pain is to deny and ignore it.

In feminist thinking death and life are *equally* important opposites in the great rhythms of nature. Feminists respect and celebrate nature as she is; we do not wish to dominate her. You do not have to believe literally in reincarnation in order to have a more dialectical, rhythmic view of life. You do need an appreciation of the sense in which one death or ending is also the beginning or birth of something else. Nothing completely disappears: people, things, energies and even ideas simply get transformed into other forms. Ultimately everything is a part of the dance of life, the great play of endless energies. This model has much in common with Eastern philosophies, as well as similarities with the modern physicist's view of the universe, in which everything is interconnected.

This way of thinking in itself can help people to cope more comfortably with death and partings. There may be a place for the counsellor to share some ideas and images of the feminist concepts of the interconnectedness of life and death, humans and nature. She may play an educational role at this stage, even suggesting some books for the departing client to read.

Dealing with the Parting
There is still the pain of parting itself. It can help if the client feels that she is taking with her something of the counsellor. She may be able to 'internalize' the counsellor, so that when faced with new situations she thinks 'What would X say?' She may have internalized the feeling of self-confidence that the counsellor gave her. When feeling low, she may remember encouraging remarks that the counsellor made. What she has learnt from counselling stays with her; she is not leaving everything behind. An image of the counsellor can feel like an internal guide, a part of the self that watches what is going on from a slight distance. The internalized counsellor might say 'There you go again with the old pattern of avoidance, attack or passivity.' As the client goes about her daily business, she is more able to notice patterns, and this is usually a first step to changing them. She can do this on her own when the 'internalized' counsellor feels really at home.

For many clients the time to end counselling sessions is when the client feels she has internalized those aspects of the counselling sessions that she wants to keep. These may include a more genuine self-respect, more self-acceptance and confidence, as well as new ways of understanding and looking at the self and others. The client needs to feel a more whole person before she can comfortably separate from the counsellor. She no longer sees the counsellor as all-good or all-powerful and herself as bad and powerless. She is able to tolerate ambiguity and the two-sidedness of people and life more easily. But it is unlikely that she will have accepted all sides of herself, even after a long period of counselling. People do not suddenly become 'perfect' whole people after lifetimes of living out certain limiting patterns. Indeed, by the time she feels ready to leave, the client usually stops expecting a total and dramatic transformation into a completely different person. This disappointment and accept-ance of the self *as it is* is a vital part of the process of counselling.

However dramatic changes do often occur. Previously timid and depressed women do blossom and follow new interests in life. Har-dened and bitter career women soften and accept more of their vulnerable sides. They may even change physically, as when a tense face relaxes. Sometimes women start sitting noticeably more upright. Such changes are particularly rewarding for the counsellor, but she needs to believe firmly in the importance of everyone's individual journey and its many stages, and to accept whatever changes have occurred as being right at that time for that particular client. Counsel-lors can become disappointed and even blame themselves when clients do not change as much or in the ways they would like. These feelings can be especially intense towards the end of counselling. There is always so much more 'work' to do. Counsellors may be afraid that without their help the client may 'slip back', or that they should offer, even insist on, more sessions. Counsellors need to investigate why they are feeling this way. Do they not trust the client? Do they feel that only they can help her? Do they feel that *they* haven't done enough? Or do they 'objectively' believe that the client needs more sessions to complete the present counselling cycle? The counsellor too needs to be able to 'let go' and trust the process.

Facing Losses
Yet this awareness of the cyclical processes of life and death, starting and ending, includes the full facing of death, loss and endings. And when a client finishes counselling these losses need to be acknow-ledged. The first loss is the loss of containment. At first the client was contained by the counsellor, who provided a safe place for the client's personal explorations. Now that particular containment will no lon-ger be available. The client will be leaving behind the security of the womb-like nature of the counselling sessions; in other words, she will be giving birth to a new stage of herself. The old stage, which usually has a childish, clinging element, is dying. The client has to leave the womb, and like the new-born baby, she needs to incorporate some aspects of that original state into her new life. The counsellor can help

her to explore ways in which she can contain herself, make her own spaces for self-exploration, and most importantly find within herself a safe place. Some counsellors use guided fantasy exercises to help the client find an imaginary 'safe place' in their heads. It might be their bed at home, or even the counselling room. The important thing is that they can 'take' this image with them to use whenever they need to. But at a deeper level the client needs to feel safe enough within her own being, to be able to contain all the powerful feelings that might emerge in future life. By showing her that she is ready to leave counselling, the counsellor is also telling the client that she can now contain herself. The client *can* cope.

The second loss is of the unconditional acceptance that the counsellor gave her. Outside in the 'real' world most people, including parents and partners, only accept us on certain conditions, such as 'only when we please them' or 'only when we are strong'. When a client leaves counselling she will no longer have the certainty of the counsellor's unconditional acceptance, so she needs to take that acceptance with her. She needs to be able to accept herself, for no one else will necessarily do it for her. In a deep sense this particular loss is a great gain for the client.

The third loss is the loss of structured time for the self. For many clients their weekly sessions are the only regular times in their lives that are solely devoted to themselves. Feminist counsellors are particularly concerned that their clients find regular times, just for themselves, during the week. It may be possible to put aside a time to write a diary every day, or meditate or just be still and with oneself. It is often very difficult for people in our culture just to *be*; they feel that they should always be *doing* something.

For some clients, group therapy or a women's consciousness-raising group, or for men a men's group might replace the counselling sessions when individual work is no longer necessary.

The fourth loss is of a very intimate relationship with a special person. The degree of intimacy involved in a good counselling relationship is often greater even than that in a good marriage or partnership. There is frequently enormous sadness at parting, a sadness shared by the counsellor too. Tears may be shed, presents exchanged. Both people often share the fact that they will miss each other. It is important to face this sadness rather than avoid it, as so many clients prefer to do. It is always important to have a final session with a client in order to face the reality of parting. If clients try to just disappear or simply write to say they are leaving, counsellors need to insist on one final meeting. As we have already noted, it is a pattern with many people to avoid saying 'proper' goodbyes, with all the pain that is so often involved. If partings are not faced then it is so much harder for the client to move on to the next stage. The person who acknowledges the pain of leaving childish dependence behind is far more likely to grow.

Accepting Gains

It seems that the most helpful transitions are those in which there is a balance between feelings of loss and feelings of anticipation for the future. It is often the case that feelings of grief and loss need to be experienced first before the person can fully experience the anticipation. When the loss is denied it tends to remain in the unconscious, poisoning the sense of independence in the new phase. Like all other opposites in the feminist model, loss and gain, dependence and independence, parting and meeting are all seen as two sides of the same coins. One opposite can only exist with the presence of the other. There can be no gain without loss.

On a purely practical level, leaving counselling means that the client gains extra time during the week, has more money in her pocket and has learnt some new skills and ways of seeing. She is embarking on a new phase of her journey equipped with more useful tools. But there is also the gain of independence, of not needing the counsellor any more. There is the gain of the sense of self-containment, self-respect and self-understanding. Perhaps there is even a sense of freedom, of not having to please anyone else. Many clients feel as if they have 'grown up'.

Counselling as a Rite of Passage

What do we mean by the words 'grown up'? Many clients who begin counselling seem to be in some way not fully separated from their parents. They are living their lives for their parents, as when their choice of career is 'what Daddy would have liked'. Or they got married 'to please Mummy'. Or they are still rebelling against parents. They have not grown into themselves, have not become who they really are. It does not mean that they have not played the role of 'grown up' as our society proscribes it.

As modern Western society lacks rituals of passage from childhood or adolescence into adulthood, people have tried to use rituals such as marriage, passing the driving test, going to college or getting a job as passports to the world of 'proper' grown-up adulthood. For men there can be a certain validity in these rites of passage, as the world they are entering is still generally male-dominated. But for women the irony is that the main rite of passage into that world, marriage, is an institution usually geared towards *preventing* the full development of women. So the very moment that a woman is supposed to be most acceptable to the adult world is also the moment when she is thrust most forcefully back into dependence and 'childishness'. Women's status in the 'real' adult world is still largely dependent on marriage and has little to do with her own personal achievements.

Counselling can be seen as an alternative kind of rite of passage to help women and men pass through the transition from 'child' to 'adult', from 'half' person to whole person, from living only in other people's terms to living as oneself. It is a way of separating from the everyday adult world, with its set role expectations and demands. All transitional rites require some form of separation from the ordinary world. They, like counselling, also involve going through a number of painful and difficult confrontations with the self. The counselling 'rite' involves reclaiming and accepting hidden parts of the self as it actually is, not as the client or her society might like her to be. And then it involves emerging back into the 'real' world and being more assertive and adult in that world.

For women in the traditional world where marriage is the only socially acceptable destiny, becoming an adult constricts and narrows the choices she has available; while becoming an adult through counselling involves an opening up of possibilities and increases her choice. Whereas in the traditional way of becoming an adult the woman has to fit herself in with a husband and later children, often *losing* her sense of self in the process, becoming an adult through counselling *increases* her sense of self.

Becoming an adult is a rite of passage that may happen many times in one lifetime. Each cycle of growth and/or counselling may involve becoming an adult in a different way, leaving some different aspect of non-separation or dependence behind and facing some new aspect of the self. And it does not mean leaving behind forever the 'child' aspects of the self. People still need to be nurtured, depend on others sometimes, act spontaneously, feel passions and pains. But each time the 'rite of passage' occurs the client will be better able to understand and use the so-called 'child' energies consciously. She will be able to know when she needs to be looked after like a child and ask assertively for such care. She will be able to recognize strong feelings of anger or jealousy without being overwhelmed by them.

Without the energies, needs and drives of our 'child' side we would be mere robots, not flesh and blood human beings. So becoming adult does not mean becoming a cold, calculating, totally logical being. It means being able to flow with the rhythms of life between the hundreds of opposite states that make up nature, with awareness, both apart and a part, both in control and letting go. It means being true to yourself.

The Last Session

The last session can be seen as the final ritual in the rite of passage that we call counselling. It may be helpful to start discussing endings after the middle phase of counselling, when the client seems to have accepted herself more, and is beginning to express 'new' sides to herself. The counsellor could suggest that they might think about an ending date that does not necessarily mean a total break for ever. The client may need to discuss the whole idea of ending and come to accept it before reaching a final decision. The counsellor could explain the options, such as returning at a later date if she feels the need.

For many clients the mere possibility of returning is enough to help them to stop coming and move on. Most never do return; but for other clients I am seen as a guide to be returned to at crucial transition periods in their journeys. They may come for a few months initially and then years later return for a few more sessions. Other clients write to me about their journeys after they have stopped counselling and keep contact that way. Sometimes a single session is arranged for a later date. Other clients choose to start coming less often before they finally finish. They may start coming only once every two weeks or even once a month before finally leaving.

Towards the end there is often a kind of 'regression' when suddenly all the old problems seem to have returned, worse then ever. This may be related to a fear of 'getting better' and therefore having to leave the counsellor. The reassurance that they can return later often helps.

The last session can be used as an opportunity to review the counselling and summarize the insights gained. Both client and counsellor can contribute to this review process, but it is important that the client does not feel judged by the counsellor or herself. Our education system is so full of marking procedures and concepts of success and failure that even confident and aware people may wonder if they have 'failed' or 'succeeded' at counselling.

There will always be more 'work' to do. Certain themes or recurring patterns of behaviour may be mentioned in this session for the client to continue working on by herself. For example, one client had come to a much clearer understanding of the way she was always trying to please people to get the approval that she never had from her mother. She accepted that her actual mother might never approve of her, whatever she did. She confronted the pain of this insight and also began practising at being more assertive in our sessions. After six months we both decided that it was time to stop. She felt much more self-accepting, and had changed her job. She was much busier now and didn't feel that she needed to come any more. But on the last session we agreed that she was still busy pleasing people a lot of the time. Her behaviour pattern hadn't changed enough, despite the new insight. We recognized that it would take a long time to change a lifetime's pattern, but she would watch herself every day and notice placatory behaviour. She suggested that a diary would help, and thought that an assertion training workshop would be useful. And we worked out some 'affirmations' to say every morning, such as 'I am a valuable, worthwhile person and deserve good things.'

I also told her that if she felt the need to return for some further sessions I would be available. As the counsellor I was playing the role of the kind mother who is still present in the background even though the child has 'grown up' and left home. I do not just disappear.

Julia

It was quite difficult even to talk about ending counselling with Julia, as she was so afraid of rejection. At the same time, she was quite passive and seemed to be waiting for me to make any major decisions about counselling. We did seem to have come to the end of a cycle as she acknowledged her emotional needs and began to be more assertive about expressing them. One day after about a year she said that she thought she could manage with only seeing me once every two weeks. 'I don't want to stop coming', she said, as though that were the worst thought imaginable. I asked her why the idea felt so awful. She didn't really know. Gradually it emerged that her main fear was that by leaving she would hurt me. It would seem as though she was rejecting me. Up to this point most of our work together had been concerned with her own fear of being rejected by other people, and how this fear had stopped her acknowledging her own needs.

Through discussing an ending we had now come across her own rejection of others. Perhaps, I wondered, there was a part of her that wanted to reject me. Perhaps a part of Julia did want to say that she thought counselling was all rubbish and I was a useless counsellor and so she was 'jolly well going to leave.' All that passivity and waiting for me to act was connected with a deep resentment that only talk of parting could bring to the surface. Partings often bring up angry feelings towards the other person. Even if it was not their decision, they may get 'blamed' for the separation. Was this connected, in Julia's case, with feelings about being abandoned by her mother? She was still so angry with her mother that just the thought of leaving me reminded her of those old feelings.

At first Julia hotly denied this interpretation, but after a while she burst into tears and agreed that yes, she was angry and did want to reject other people, including me. But she quickly added: 'But I don't really want to reject you; you haven't done anything bad to me.' In Julia's mind endings and rejections had become completely entwined. She could not even imagine an ending that was not a rejection. Because she realized the time to finish counselling was approaching, she was terrified of both rejecting and being rejected by me.

For a couple of sessions we looked at the part of her that wanted to reject me. She imagined that I had suggested that it was time to end, although in fact I had not. Julia felt that I wanted to get rid of her. When I asked why she thought I might want to get rid of her, she quickly said 'Because you're bored with me.' We looked at each other, and spontaneously we both burst out laughing. Her response had been so quick and certain, Of course she must be so boring that I couldn't wait to get rid of her! Another part of Julia knew that she was not boring and that in fact I was not bored with her at all. I am sure she sensed that I found her a very interesting and frequently rewarding client.

This burst of laughter released a realization in Julia that actually I wasn't rejecting her, and she then said: 'I'm not rejecting you either. It's just that I'd like to have a deadline for finishing that I can work towards. And I need to know that if I want to continue after that, it will be OK.' She was now taking the ending into her own hands; she had stopped being so passive. She had defined clearly and assertively what she wanted, and by admitting that she wanted a definite date to end she was inevitably rejecting me. In fact when the day came for Julia to finish she seemed quite determined that this was the right decision. She told me that she didn't feel that she had to please me by only telling me about the 'good' she had gained from counselling, or that she now felt completely 'cured'. She analysed what she had learnt very clearly and described the main change as admitting that she had emotional needs associated with her body as well as her mind. She said that acknowledging that she actually had a body was one of the most important new experiences for her. Julia also felt that she didn't need either of her parents' approval any more, especially her father's. She realized that mental and academic achievement was not the only important thing in life.

But Julia did feel that she was still afraid of rejection, and that it would take her a long time to stop having this fear. It was also clear that she was rejecting others. I suggested that this was an area she could work on after finishing counselling with me. She could notice when she rejected others and examine the reasons, maybe even write them down. We discussed the possibility that one day she might wish to return to counselling either with me or someone else to go 'deeper' into her feelings about her mother and abandonment. This seemed to be the next theme or cycle that she could work with when ready. But first she needed to consolidate her new-found physical confidence and sense of being grounded in her own body.

She had already started doing yoga and this seemed to be an important next step. She was making a lot of time for herself, painting and meditating. Julia was also going to parties again and dancing, which was yet another way of expressing her body. She was still afraid of sexual encounters with either men or women, but told me that the idea seemed more acceptable now and she was letting herself be attracted to men more easily, without immediately dismissing them, or rejecting them as 'not OK'.

On the last day Julia brought me a painting as a farewell present. She waited until she was about to leave and then gave it to me. We were both rather tearful at this point and gave each other a big hug. Then she rushed off at speed down the street.

A few months later I received a long letter from Julia telling me that she had moved with some friends to the country, was teaching and painting and had just started a sexual relationship with a 'wonderful' woman.

Mary

Mary had originally asked for a limited number of sessions to help with her depression and difficulties sleeping. We had started with six weeks and then increased to eighteen weeks. She had been worried about money and did not feel that she could afford much more than eighteen weeks. But as the time to end drew nearer, she began to get quite anxious. She had always been so used to having someone to lean on, and for the past three months I had been that person. She was terrified of ending and being completely alone, even though in the middle phase of counselling she had faced the fact that we are all ultimately alone. Her original symptoms of depression and poor sleeping had both lifted as she began 'standing up' for herself more, being angry and setting clear boundaries, but two weeks before she was due to finish she complained that she was feeling depressed again and her sleeping was once more badly disturbed. I asked her how she felt about leaving. She claimed at first that she didn't mind and hadn't got enough money for any more sessions anyway. I told her that we could extend the sessions and there were a number of alternative ways in which we could organize them. In her typically passive way, Mary had assumed that once-a-week counselling at the set price was the only alternative available. This was similar to the way she had assumed the style of her marriage was the only possible style.

The opening up of alternative possibilities and choices in relation to counselling gave her a feeling of relief and freedom that she later told me had helped her in other areas. Eventually we decided that she would come every two weeks and would pay a little less than she had been paying. This new arrangement worked well. And she would usually have 'assertiveness tasks' as 'homework' to do in the intervening week. This arrangement went on for nearly a year, during which Mary became much more assertive. Her relationship with her husband was still not good, however, and she felt that either they had to separate or they should get some counselling together. When she came to tell me this decision she seemed sad, but clear that it had to be one or the other. She asked me if I could see both of them, I told her that I was *her* counsellor. I was there only for her, and it would be better for them to see someone else as a couple. I recommended someone who they went to see, and arranged a series of sessions with. Mary then told me that they could not afford both kinds of counselling, and therefore wanted to finish with me but make a single appointment for a later date. I agreed to this, but asked first whether she was putting their relationship above herself, in denying herself the sessions with me. She didn't think so.

At first I was unsure about Mary's decision, but when she came to see me two months later it was clear that the counselling had been helpful, and in fact she and her husband had now decided amicably to separate. She looked like a different person, and sat up much straighter in her chair. She was tanned and had put on a little weight. The relief in her whole body was obvious. She thanked me profusely for all my help, and although this thanking did feel a bit placatory, I accepted it and shared my sense of how different she looked. Mary was going to move away, too. I told her that if she ever wanted to contact me and come back for some sessions, she would be welcome. We also parted with a big hug.

Louise

Louise told me that she realized that by staying in her marriage she was limiting herself in terms of personal growth. 'I can't change any more; it's gone far enough' was the kind of thing she kept saying to me. I asked her what kinds of changes in her she imagined would take place if she didn't stay in her marriage. She was vague and unclear about any alternative future, and it was clear that she had made up her mind. At this point she began to close off from me. It was as if any further change was just too threatening and I had become rather like a devil figure whom she feared might entice her into 'evil' ways.

One day she asked me whether I was a feminist and asked what exactly that meant. I explained a little and reassured her that it didn't mean that I hated men, but she did not seem convinced. I felt disappointed that our originally very trusting and warm relationship appeared to have changed. Louise was erecting some pretty firm barriers, and it felt almost as though I was now the enemy. I realized this was partly a way of coping with her decision to stay with an oppressive husband, despite the other side of her which was crying out to leave. She needed to see things in all-or-nothing terms of 'good' and 'bad' right now, in order to remain with her decision. She was also genuinely wary of what the media presented as feminism. Like many other women, especially those in traditional marriages or just traditional environments, Louise was afraid that her own development and rebellion would be disapproved of by her family and friends. She feared the break-up of her family as a result. And the word 'feminism' had been associated in her mind with 'man-hating lesbians'. Louise told me that she didn't want to end up 'like that'. When I suggested that there might be many other alternatives between traditional marriage and separatist lesbian life, she changed the subject as though she just didn't want to hear.

I told her that I respected her decision and wondered why she was feeling so angry with me at the moment. At first she denied any anger, but then burst out with 'It's all right for you to be all independent and live without men. You're middle-class. I'm not, and we just don't live like that. I don't need you telling me what to do.' She had assumed that I was actually telling her that she should leave her husband. I had never said that, and I was somewhat taken aback at the outburst, but there seemed little point in refuting her accusation when I admitted to myself that I did think she should leave. It had been a relief when she spoke, as I had felt something brewing for weeks. She apologized afterwards and I agreed that there was a real difference in our situations. She was right about that, but it was her life we were interested in, not mine.

After this session Louise said that she wanted to end the counselling. She told me that it had been very helpful: she had stopped compulsively eating and that was a massive achievement. She also said that she was much clearer now about her own needs and would make sure that these got met now. She brought me some flowers on our last session. I thought that these might be partly her way of saying 'sorry' as well as being a goodbye gift. But there was still a strained distance between us, and I had a strong sense of there being much unfinished business. Yet I respected her decision to leave at that point, and told myself to trust the process and have faith in her ability to travel her own journey in her own way and in her own time. I was not indispensable to that journey.

We have followed Julia, Mary and Louise through one cycle of their journeys, knowing that for each of them there will be more cycles to come. By using the 'feminine' model of cycles and rhythms I hope to have shown a different way of thinking about counselling and personal growth. This model of interconnected, ever-changing opposites differs deeply from the prevailing model of divided, split opposites and its over-emphasis on winning or losing.

Feminist counselling can help women and men too from all walks of life to shed the old models of thinking and live more satisfying lives. As we have seen, it can encourage them to discover and then 'dance' to their own rhythms of life, rather than always be marching to another's beat.

But it can also help to prepare people for living in a more fluid and unpredictable world in which the rhythm model of constant change may be a useful tool in helping us to cope. The old control model has become too rigid and all-embracing, long outliving its usefulness and helping to lead the human race towards self-destruction. There is no more total control than the ability to destroy totally; we may need to turn to new and less hierarchical ways of thinking for our very survival. Feminist counselling can also play a vital part in empowering people, and developing more equal relationships between human beings, leading to a more genuinely democratic society.

References

Adler, A. (1956) *The Individual Psychology of Alfred Adler*, ed. H. and R. Ansbacher. New York: Basic Books.

Baker-Miller, J. (1978) *Towards a New Psychology of Women*. Harmondsworth: Penguin.

Berlotti, E. (1977) *Little Girls*. London: Readers and Writers Co-operative.

Brown, L. and Liss-Levinson, N. (1981) 'Feminist Therapy', in R. Corsini (ed.), *Handbook of Innovative Psychotherapies*. New York: Wiley.

Capra, F. (1975) *The Tao of Physics*. Berkeley, CA: Shambhala.

Capra, F. (1982) *The Turning Point*. London: Wildwood House.

Chesler, P. (1972) *Women and Madness*. New York: Avon.

Chodorow, N. (1978) *The Reproduction of Mothering*. California: University of California Press.

Daly, M. (1986) *Beyond God the Father*. London: Women's Press.

d'Ardenne, Patricia (forthcoming) *Transcultural Counselling in Action*. London: Sage.

De Beauvoir, S. (1960) *The Second Sex*. London: Jonathan Cape.

Dickson, A. (1982) *A Woman in Your Own Right*. London: Quartet.

Engels, F. (1934) *Dialectics of Nature*. Moscow: Progress Publishers.

English, D. and Ehrenreich B. (1979) *For her Own Good*. London: Pluto.

Firestone, S. (1979) *The Dialectic of Sex*. London: Women's Press.

Forisba, B. (1981) 'Feminist Therapy', in R. Corsini (ed.), *Handbook of Innovative Therapies*. New York: Wiley.

Friedan, B. (1977) *The Feminine Mystique*. New York: Dell.

Gibran, K. (1972) *The Prophet*. London: Heinemann.

Gimbutas, M. (1982) *The Goddesses and Gods of Old Europe*. London: Thames and Hudson.

Graves, R. (1955) *The Greek Myths*, vols 1 and 2. Harmondsworth: Pelican.

Greer, G. (1971) *The Female Eunuch*. London: Paladin.

Hall, N. (1980) *The Moon and the Virgin*. London: Women's Press.

Horney, K. (1924) 'On the Genesis of the Castration Complex in Women', *International Journal of Psychoanalysis*, 5. Reprinted in Horney, *Feminine Psychology*. London: Routledge & Kegan Paul, 1967.

Lao Tsu (1972) *Tao te Ching*, tr. Gia-fu Feng and J. English. London: Wildwood House.

Melaart, J. (1963) 'Deities and Shrines of Neolithic Anatolia', *Archeology*, 16 (1): 29–38.

Melaart, J. (1967) *Catal Huyak, a Neolithic Town in Anatolia*. London: Thames and Hudson.

Mitchell, J. (1975) *Psychoanalysis and Feminism*. Harmondsworth: Penguin.

Orbach, S., and Eichenbaum, L. (1982) *Outside in, Inside Out*. Harmondsworth: Penguin.

Orbach, S., and Eichenbaum, L. (1983) *What do Women Want?* London: Pelican.

Orbach, S., and Eichenbaum, L. (1985) *Understanding Women*. London: Pelican.

Perara, S. (1981) *Descent to the Goddess*. Toronto: Inner City Books.

Purce, J. (1974) *The Mystic Spiral — Journey of the Soul*. London: Thames and Hudson.

Reich, J. (1970) *The Mass Psychology of Fascism*. London: Pelican.

Rogers, C. (1951) *Client Centered Therapy*. Boston, MA: Houghton Miffin.

Ryan, J. (1983) *Feminism and Therapy*. London: Polytechnic of North London.

Starhawk (1982) *Dreaming the Dark*. Boston: Beacon Press.

Steiner, C. and Wycoff, H. (1975) *Readings in Radical Psychiatry*. New York: Grove Press.

Stone, M. (1976) *When God was a Woman*. New York: Harcourt Brace Jovanovich.

Index

abandonment, experiences of 58, 59, 91,
    112, 119, 121
acceptance
    of client 19, 28, 30, 31, 35–8, 44, 78,
        83–4, 115
    of others 89
    of self 52, 62–3, 72–3, 75, 77, 80, 84,
        85, 90, 110, 112–14
acting, in counselling 17
Adler, A. 21
advertising, pressures from 37, 49, 108
advice, and counselling 18, 37
agency, state, as controlling 21
aggression
    compared with assertion 98–9
    male 92, 97
ambivalence
    accepting 39, 43, 71–84
    towards counsellor 72–6, 83–4, 114
anger
    expression of 8, 57, 68, 75–6, 78–9,
        82–3, 86, 100–1, 104, 117
    repression of 53–4, 65–7, 70
anima/animus 17
archetypes 37–9
art therapy 17
assertion, encouragement of 8, 17, 88,
    97, 119
assertiveness
    as 'masculine' value 3
    sexual 104–5
    training 14, 16–17, 98–110, 119, 122
        techniques 100–4
association, free 61, 64
attention, to client 19, 36–7
attitudes, social 9–10

Baker-Miller, J. 16
behaviour
    as learned 16
    unlearning 62
black women 24
Blake, William 44

blame, externalizing 8
    see also guilt, feelings of
bodies, women's attitudes to 9, 47
body, awareness/acceptance of 28–30,
    41–2, 94–5, 99, 106–7, 120–1
body language, in assertiveness training
    100–1
body work, in counselling 26, 95
boundaries, stating 101–2, 106, 108
broken record technique, in
    assertiveness training 102, 105, 108

Capra, F. 85
change
    asking for 100–2
    strategies for 87–97
    see also assertiveness, training
child, see parent/child, as opposites
childhood, experiences 14, 15, 42–3, 57–
    70, 81, 105
children, humiliation of 32, 41, 46, 59
churches, counselling services 20
class, and access to counselling 21–2
cleanliness, attitudes to 34–5
client, role of 7, 18, 36
client-centred approach 16
co-counselling 18
communication, patriarchal structures
    98
confrontation, in counselling 41
consciousness-raising, groups 18–19, 26,
    50, 115
containing, see holding
control
    client's need for 45, 47, 48, 50, 55, 77
    see also rhythms, of control/letting go
'control model' 4–6, 9, 45–6, 125
co-operation, as 'feminine' value 3
counselling
    directive 63–4
    formal/informal 18–20
    non-directive 62–3

counselling, feminist
definition 2–4
influences on 10–15
social limits of 15–16
techniques 8, 16–17, 26, 61–4
counsellor
client's ambivalence towards 72–6
role of 7, 14, 18, 23, 26–7, 36, 62–4,
88–9, 95–6
in assertiveness training 105–6
couple counselling 91, 122
criticism, impact of 35–6, 42–3, 53, 68,
104–5
crying 37, 65, 76, 80–2, 97
cycles
in ancient mythologies 10–11
in counselling process 1

Daly, M. 1
dancing, in counselling 17
deadlines, pre-arranged 111
death, as image 85–7
defences, valuing 41–3
dependency, feelings of 48, 76
depression
in middle phase 87
as reason for referral 33
desires, acknowledging 79, 81–2, 86, 89,
94–5, 105
detachment, of counsellor 19–20
development, cycles of 3, 86–7
dialectics 12
Dickson, A. 17, 98
dirt, fear of 37–8, 91
dominance, in sexual relations 92
drawing, in counselling 17, 95
dreams, in counselling 17, 39, 68–9, 75,
95

eating problems
and need for control 47, 50
as reason for referral 33–4, 45, 54, 68
Eliot, T.S. 56
empathy, of counsellor 16, 20
Engels, Friedrich 12
envy, of counsellor 23, 79, 81, 84
equality
need for in counselling 23–5, 26, 76,
88
of other, in assertion 100–1
expectations, client 25–6

failure, patterns of 33
family, splits in 59–60
fantasy
guided 17, 61, 64, 81–2, 115
and reality, accepting 85
father, influence of 8, 30, 51–2, 68–9, 80
fathering, at first interview 25
feedback, from counsellor 31, 34, 43,
62–3, 79
feelings
expression of 76–7, 80–2, 99
strategies for 77–80
repression of 9, 19
'female', 'feminine' 2–3, 10, 17, 28
feminism
clients' attitude to 122–3
modern 12–13
Freud, Sigmund 13–14

gain, acceptance of 116
Gestalt therapy 15
Gibran, Khalil 108
Gimbutas, M. 11
giving/receiving 89–90
goals, of client 44–5, 55
god, as male 9
goddess, multiform 11, 86, 99
'grounding' exercises 94
group therapy 115
guilt, feelings of 56–7, 69, 96–7, 104,
108–9

Hall, N. 17, 28, 99
harassment, sexual 8, 103
healing, and women 12
health, alternative approaches to 20,
32–3
hierarchy
counsellor/client 1, 7, 14, 15, 23, 72,
73
inner 62–4, 67–70
acceptance of 71–84
in 'masculine' thought 3–4, 6, 9–10,
24–5, 41, 50, 59–60, 74
social 34–5, 43, 45–7
transformation of 7
holding
in counselling 7, 31, 36–7, 42, 44–5,
53, 78, 97, 114–15
of feelings 78, 115

holism
  in education 59
  in humanistic psychology 15
home, working from 22–3
Horney, Karen 13
hostility, to counsellor 73–5

ideologies, feminist 17
images, in counselling 17, 85–7
independence
  as 'masculine' value 3, 48
  through counselling 83, 91, 97, 116
inferiority, feelings of 67–8
interconnection
  in ancient mythologies 10–11
  in 'feminine' thought 3–4, 7, 10, 12,
    20, 125
intimacy, desire for 46–7

jealousy 33, 66, 117
Judeo-Christianity, sex and sin in 56–7
Julia
  assertiveness training 106–8
  endings 119–21
  final stage 94–5
  first stage 30–1, 33, 37, 39, 41–2
  middle stage 80–2, 94
  second stage 51–3
  third stage 64–6
June, middle stage 86
Jung, C.G. 9, 17, 37–8, 93

labyrinth, as symbol of counselling 57–8,
  78
Lao Tsu 71
laughter, value of 42
lesbians 24, 107
listening 16, 18, 25, 32, 37, 78
location 22–4
loss, coping with 114–16
Louise
  assertiveness training 109–10
  endings 122–3
  final stage 96–7
  first stage 33–6, 37, 38–9, 43
  middle stage 83–4
  second stage 54–5
  third stage 60–1, 68–70

'male', 'masculine' 2–3, 10
marriage
  expectations of 57

traditional 35, 110, 116–17, 122–3
Marx, Karl 12
Mary
  assertiveness training 108–9
  endings 121–2
  final stage 95–6
  first stage 31–3, 37, 39, 42–3
  middle stage 82–3, 95, 121
  second stage 53–4
  third stage 66–8
masturbation 107
memories, earliest 61, 64
men
  expression of feelings 77
  and 'mothering' 28
men's groups 115
menstruation
  attitudes to 35
  and physical rhythms 92–3
middle age, changes in 93
mind/body hierarchy 9, 29, 46, 49, 51–2,
  94
Mitchell, Juliet 13
mother
  abandonment by 58, 59
  as 'good' and 'bad' 39–40, 43, 65, 69–
    70, 81
  as symbol 37–40
mothering
  in counselling 25, 28–43, 51, 53, 119
  devaluation of 28–9, 38
  holding 36–7
  letting go 37
  see also acceptance
mourning, for 'perfect' partner 74–6,
  83

neglect, feelings of 60, 65
negotiation 96, 102, 108
nurturing
  as 'female' value 3, 20, 89–90
  need for 25, 50, 54–5

opposites
  conflicting 46–9
    accepting 71–84
    balancing 89–97
    expressing 98–110
    identifying 49–53, 62
  interconnection of 3–4, 6, 7, 10, 12,
    20, 36, 125

opposites — *cont.*
  internalization of 59
Orbach, S. and Eichenbaum, L. 13–14

parent
  counsellor as 7, 14, 23, 25, 38, 74–5,
    88
    see also mothering
  perfect, idea of 74–6, 79, 83, 85
parent/child, as opposites 9, 30, 46, 48,
    49, 55, 63–4, 79, 83–4, 117
parents
  anger towards 57
  influence of 59–60
parting
  coping with 111–12, 115–16, 119–23
  feminist approach 113–14
past, influence of 56–70
patriarchy 3, 21, 36–7, 46, 48, 51–2, 57,
    70, 80, 99, 103
  and devaluation of mothering 28–9
patterns
  in counselling 47, 48, 112
  identifying 44–5, 52, 58, 61, 65–6, 72,
    113–14, 118–19
payment 26, 121–2
Perera, S. 6
perfection, striving for 49, 51
persecution, experiences of 32, 80
persecutor, men in role of 32
Persephone/Demeter/Hecate myth 11,
    29
personal/political, in feminist
    counselling 21
power/powerlessness 9, 48–9, 55, 67–70,
    83–4
power structures 13, 36, 60
pre-menstrual tension 92
pressure, social 44–5, 108
prioritizing, as categorizing 'male'
    thought 3
problem-solver, counsellor as 96–7
projections 40, 41, 80, 88
psyche, as interconnected with body 4
psychoanalysis 13–14, 16, 21
psychology, humanistic 15, 16

racism 2, 80
rage
  expressing 40, 43, 75–6
  feelings of 31, 32, 60, 66

rationalization 41–2
realities, objective/subjective 7–10, 14,
    36
rebirth, as image 86–7
rebirthing 15
referrals 20–2, 24
regression 118
Reich, J. 21
rejection
  accepting use of 89, 119–20
  by counsellor 38, 76, 112
  experiences of 38, 50–2, 60, 64, 80,
    107, 119
  fear of 46–7
relationships
  and assertiveness training 106–7
  and rhythm model 72
relaxation, teaching 88, 94–5
remothering 31, 36
resentment, feelings of 60, 67, 119
rhythm, in ancient mythologies 10–12
'rhythm model' 4–6, 9, 12, 20, 71–2, 125
  and counselling 7, 41, 58
rhythms
  of control/letting go 4, 37, 91–4, 96–7
  emotional 89–90
  life/death 112–13
  lifestyle 93–4, 112
  physical 92–3
  relational 90–1
rite of passage, counselling as 116–17,
    118
Rogers, C. 16
role-play, use of 100
Ryan, J. 23

sadness, accepting 10, 65, 71–2, 82–3
self-confidence, development of 7, 33,
    104–5, 113
self-esteem, low 7, 8, 22, 43, 50–1, 58,
    75, 101, 105
self-help groups 15, 18–19, 26
  see also consciousness-raising groups
separation
  from children 108–9
  as part of growing up 46–7, 50–1, 52,
    59, 69, 83, 86, 111–12, 116–17
sexuality
  and assertiveness 104–5
  problems with 92
  repression of 70

'shadow, the' 9
silence, in interview 31–2, 42, 51, 77–8
skills, social 25
snake, as image of wisdom 11–12
socializing, client/counsellor 26–7
space, personal 9, 93–4, 95–6, 108, 115
spiral
    as symbol of movement in counselling
        3, 44, 72, 78, 86–7, 111
    as symbol of wisdom 11–12, 20
stages of counselling 1–2
    ending 111–24
    final 87–97
    first 25–6, 30–6, 44
    middle 72–84, 85–7, 91, 112, 118
    second 44–55
    third 56–70
    see also assertiveness, training
Starhawk 111
status
    and marriage 116–17
    second-class, of women 4, 16, 29, 38,
        46, 50
stereotyping, gender 4
strategies, coping 16
supporter, counsellor as 96–7
symbols
    use of 17, 95
    see also mother, as symbol

Taoism, influence of 15
teacher, counsellor as 64, 88, 95–6, 113

themes
    identifying 44–55, 56
    origins of 56–70
therapist, role of 14
thought, 'masculine'/'feminine' 2–3
time
    personal 115, 121
    taking, in assertiveness training 102–3
timing of sessions 26
touching, as harassment 8
transactional analysis 15
transference, in psychoanalysis 14

unconscious, social 9–10, 22
uselessness, feelings of 49, 51

values
    of counsellor 35–6, 87–8
    'masculine'/'feminine' 2–3, 28
victim, women in role of 32, 53–4, 68, 80
virgin, woman as 99
vulnerability 9, 54, 70, 83–4

weakness, fear of 9
wisdom, feminist 10–12
women's centres 21, 23, 24, 96
Women's Therapy Centre, London 13,
    23

Index compiled by Meg Davies
(Society of Indexers)

Also from SAGE Publications...

Counselling in Practice

Series Editor
Windy Dryden *Goldsmiths' College, University of London*
Associate Editor
E Thomas Dowd *Kent State University*

This is a new series of concise, practical books which focus on specific client problem areas. Developed especially for counsellors and students of counselling, the volumes transcend particular counselling approaches to explore ways of working with clients from a broad theoretical base. Each book relates the theory to practice, providing clear and explicit guidelines for the process of counselling.

Volumes include:

- **Counselling Couples**
  by **Donald Bubenzer and John West**

- **Counselling with Dreams and Nightmares**
  by **Delia Cushway and Robyn Sewell**

- **Counselling Survivors of Childhood Sexual Abuse**
  by **Claire Burke Draucker**

- **Counselling for Depression**
  by **Paul Gilbert**

- **Counselling for Anxiety Problems**
  by **Richard Hallam**

- **Career Counselling**
  by **Robert Nathan and Linda Hill**

- **Counselling for Post-Traumatic Stress Disorder**
  by **Michael J Scott and Stephen G Stradling**

- **Counselling for Alcohol Problems**
  by **Richard Velleman**

For further details, contact **SAGE Publications** at the following address:

6 Bonhill Street,
London EC2A 4PU,
England

or

PO Box 5084,
Newbury Park, CA
91359-9924, USA

Also from SAGE Publications...

Key Figures in Counselling and Psychotherapy

Series Editor
Windy Dryden *Goldsmiths' College, University of London*

This exciting and unique new series provides concise introductions to the lives, contributions and influence of the leading innovators whose theoretical and practical work has had a profound impact on counselling and psycho-therapy.

Volumes include:

- **Fritz Perls**
  by **Petrŭska Clarkson and Jennifer Mackewn**

- **Sigmund Freud**
  by **Michael Jacobs**

- **Melanie Klein**
  by **Julia Segal**

- **Eric Berne**
  by **Ian Stewart**

- **Carl Rogers**
  by **Brian Thorne**

- **Aaron Beck**
  by **Marjorie Weishaar**

- **Albert Ellis**
  by **Joe Yankura and Windy Dryden**

For further details, contact **SAGE Publications** at the following address:

6 Bonhill Street, London EC2A 4PU, England

or

PO Box 5084, Newbury Park, CA 91359-9924, USA